THE FOURFOLD GOSPEL
INTRODUCTION

THE FOURFOLD GOSPEL

SECTION I

INTRODUCTION

BY

Edwin A. Abbott

Honorary Fellow of St John's College, Cambridge

"What seek ye?"

St John i. 38
(compare Genesis xxxvii. 15)

Cambridge :
at the University Press
1913

CAMBRIDGE
UNIVERSITY PRESS

University Printing House, Cambridge CB2 8BS, United Kingdom

Published in the United States of America by Cambridge University Press, New York

Cambridge University Press is part of the University of Cambridge.

It furthers the University's mission by disseminating knowledge in the pursuit of education, learning and research at the highest international levels of excellence.

www.cambridge.org
Information on this title: www.cambridge.org/9781107418417

© Cambridge University Press 1913

This publication is in copyright. Subject to statutory exception and to the provisions of relevant collective licensing agreements, no reproduction of any part may take place without the written permission of Cambridge University Press.

First published 1913
First paperback edition 2014

A catalogue record for this publication is available from the British Library

ISBN 978-1-107-41841-7 Paperback

Cambridge University Press has no responsibility for the persistence or accuracy of URLs for external or third-party internet websites referred to in this publication, and does not guarantee that any content on such websites is, or will remain, accurate or appropriate.

TO

THOSE WHO ARE WILLING TO UNDERTAKE THE STUDY

OF THE FOUR GOSPELS

AS IMPERFECT DOCUMENTS

IN THE BELIEF THAT THEIR VERY IMPERFECTIONS

WERE PERMITTED OR ORDAINED

TO DRAW US NEARER

THROUGH THE LETTER TO THE SPIRIT

OF THE PERFECT LIFE

WHICH THEY IMPERFECTLY DESCRIBE

PREFACE

Previous Parts (published in 1900–12) of the series of which this is the tenth have dealt mostly with words. This Part will attempt to elucidate thoughts with the help of the evidence extracted from the elucidations of words. The earlier volumes might perhaps be described as a letting down of nets. If so, this one might be called an attempt to draw them in.

The "nets" were, in fact, footnotes, which, in former volumes, were very many and very long. They were also often apparently digressive. The reason was that I mostly wrote them with a view to future investigations as well as, or more than, to the matter in hand. When fishermen let down their nets, the boats that row round a shoal of fish sometimes look as though they were rowing away from it; and my boats often (I dare say) presented the appearance of rowing away from that which they were attempting to surround and capture.

Now I fear that I may incur an opposite charge. The notes in the present volume may seem too few and too slight to justify the statements placed in the text above them. If they do, I must ask the reader to remember that fishermen cannot draw nets in, and let them down, at one and the same time.

It will be found (I think) that a brief note of a line or two in the present volume—beside giving references to original authorities—often refers the reader to a discussion extending to several pages in a previous Part of Diatessarica, where the earliest authorities on the point in question are fully and accurately quoted, with so much of the context as will enable the serious student to form a judgment of their meaning. Reject my conclusions he may. Perhaps he often will. But if he does, it will be because he finds them novel, or because they seem to him fanciful or mystical, or because he thinks the evidence I have myself alleged against my own views stronger than the evidence I have alleged in support of them—not because the evidence has been unfairly, or carelessly, or inadequately collected and classified, or because it can be convicted of any suppression of inconvenient truth.

Comparing the present volume with my articles on the Gospels in the Encyclopaedia Biblica (1901) and in the Encyclopaedia Britannica (1880) and with the earliest Parts of Diatessarica, I find that the Fourth Gospel, in spite of its poetic nature, is closer to history than I had supposed. The study of it, and especially of those passages where it intervenes to explain expressions in Mark altered or omitted by Luke, appears to me to throw new light on the words, acts, and purposes of Christ, and to give increased weight to His claims on our faith and worship.

My thanks are due once more to Mr W. S. Aldis, Mr H. Candler, and Rev. J. Hunter Smith, for corrections of proof and valuable suggestions. To Mr Candler I am also indebted for trenchant criticisms of my refusal to admit that the Fourth Gospel is a mere poem. These have often been of great service by directing my attention to features in that Gospel, and to early authorities, especially in Jewish literature, which seemed to justify the position I had attributed to the Evangelist, where, without such justification, it might have incurred the charge of being "modern."

EDWIN A. ABBOTT.

Wellside, Well Walk,
Hampstead, N.W.
12 *May* 1913.

CONTENTS

CONTENTS

CHAPTER V

THE COURSE OF PROCEDURE

CHAPTER VI

"PARALEIPOMENA" OR "THINGS OMITTED"

CHAPTER VII

ORDER AND ARRANGEMENT IN HEBREW HISTORIES

CHAPTER VIII

ORDER AND ARRANGEMENT IN MARK

CONTENTS

CHAPTER IX

ORDER AND ARRANGEMENT IN MATTHEW

CHAPTER X

ORDER AND ARRANGEMENT IN LUKE

CHAPTER XI

ORDER AND ARRANGEMENT IN JOHN

REFERENCES AND ABBREVIATIONS

REFERENCES

(i) *Black Arabic numbers* refer to paragraphs in the several volumes of Diatessarica, as to which see p. 178 :—

    1— 272=*Clue.*
    273— 552=*Corrections of Mark.*
    553—1149=*From Letter to Spirit.*
    1150—1435=*Paradosis.*
    1436—1885=*Johannine Vocabulary.*
    1886—2799=*Johannine Grammar.*
    2800—2999=*Notes on New Testament Criticism.*
    3000—3635=*The Son of Man.*
    3636—3999=*Light on the Gospel from an ancient Poet.*

(ii) The Books of Scripture are referred to by the ordinary abbreviations, except where specified below. But when it is said that Samuel, Isaiah, Matthew, or any other writer, wrote this or that, it is to be understood as meaning *the writer, whoever he may be, of the words in question*, and not as meaning that the actual writer was Samuel, Isaiah, or Matthew.

(iii) The principal Greek MSS are denoted by ℵ, A, B, etc. ; the Latin versions by *a, b*, etc., as usual. The Syriac version discovered by Mrs Lewis on Mount Sinai is referred to as SS, *i.e.* "Sinaitic Syrian." It is always quoted from Prof. Burkitt's translation. I regret that in the first three vols. of Diatessarica Mrs Lewis's name was omitted in connection with this version.

(iv) The text of the Greek Old Testament adopted is that of B, edited by Prof. Swete ; of the New, that of Westcott and Hort.

(v) Modern works are referred to by the name of the work, or author, vol., and page, *e.g.* Levy iii. 343 *a, i.e.* vol. iii. p. 343, col. 1.

ABBREVIATIONS

Aq. = Aquila's version of O.T.
Brederek = Brederek's *Konkordanz zum Targum Onkelos*, Giessen, 1906.
Burk. = Prof. F. C. Burkitt's *Evangelion Da-mepharreshe*, Cambridge University Press, 1904.
Chr. = *Chronicles.*
Clem. Alex. 42 = Clement of Alexandria in Potter's page 42.
Dalman, *Words* = *Words of Jesus*, Eng. Transl. 1902 ; *Aram. G.* = *Grammatik des Jüdisch-Palästinischen Aramäisch*, 1894.
En. = Enoch ed. Charles, Clarendon Press, 1893.

Ency. = *Encyclopaedia Biblica.*
Ephrem = Ephraemus Syrus, ed. Moesinger.
Etheridge = Etheridge's translations of the Targums on the Pentateuch.
Euseb. = the Ecclesiastical History of Eusebius.
Field = Origenis Hexaplorum quae supersunt, Oxford, 1875, also Otium Norvicense, 1881.
Gesen. = the Oxford edition of Gesenius.
Goldschm. = *Der Babylonische Talmud,* 1897—1912, ed. Goldschmidt.
Hastings = Dictionary of the Bible, ed. Hastings (5 vols.).
Hor. Heb. = *Horae Hebraicae,* by John Lightfoot, 1658—74, ed. Gandell, Oxf. 1859.
Iren. = the treatise of Irenaeus against Heresies.
Jer. Targ. or Targ. Jer. (abbrev. for Jerusalem Targum), or Jon. Targ. (*i.e.* Targum of Jonathan, abbrev. for the Targum of Pseudo-Jonathan) = the Targum of Pseudo-Jonathan on the Pentateuch, of which there are two recensions—both quoted (*Notes on N.T. Criticism,* Pref. p. viii) by ancient authorities under the name "Jerusalem Targum." The two recensions are severally denoted by Jer. I and Jer. II. On other books, the Targum is referred to as simply "Targ."
Jon. Targ., see Jer. Targ.
Justin = Justin Martyr (*Apol.* = his First Apology, *Tryph.* = the Dialogue with Trypho).
K. = *Kings.* See also p. 15, n. 1.
Krauss = Krauss's *Griechische und Lateinische Lehnwörter* etc., Berlin, 1899.
Levy = Levy's *Neuhebräisches und Chaldäisches Wörterbuch,* 4 vols., Leipzig, 1889; Levy *Ch.* = *Chaldäisches Wörterbuch,* 2 vols., 1881.
L.S. = Liddell and Scott's Greek Lexicon.
Mechilta, see Wü(nsche).
Onk. = the Targum of Onkelos on the Pentateuch.
Origen is referred to variously, e.g. *Hom. Exod.* ii. 25=lib. ii. ch. 25 of Hom. Exod., but Orig. on Exod. ii. 25 = the commentary *ad loc.*; Lomm. iii. 24 = vol. iii. p. 24 of Lommatzsch's edition.
Oxf. Conc. = *The Oxford Concordance to the Septuagint.*
Pesikta, see Wü(nsche).
Philo is referred to by Mangey's volume and page, *e.g.* Philo ii. 234, or, as to Latin treatises, by the Scripture text or Aucher's pages (P. A.).
Pistis = *Pistis Sophia,* referred to by marginal pages, ed. Petermann.
Ps. Sol. = *Psalms of Solomon,* ed. Ryle and James, Cambr. 1891.
R., after Gen., Exod., Lev. etc. means *Rabboth,* and refers to Wünsche's edition of the Midrash on the Pentateuch, e.g. *Gen. r.* (on Gen. xii. 2, Wü. p. 177).
Rashi, sometimes quoted from Breithaupt's translation, 1714.
S. = *Samuel*; s. = "see."
Schöttg. = Schöttgen's *Horae Hebraicae,* Dresden and Leipzig, 1733.

REFERENCES AND ABBREVIATIONS

Sir.=the work of Ben Sira, *i.e.* the son of Sira. It is commonly called
Ecclesiasticus (see *Clue* **20** *a*). The original Hebrew used in this work is
that which has been edited, in part, by Cowley and Neubauer, Oxf. 1897;
in part, by Schechter and Taylor, Cambr. 1899 ; in part, by G. Margoliouth,
Jewish Quart. Rev., Oct. 1899 (also printed in *About Hebrew Manu-
scripts* (Frowde, 1905) by Mr E. N. Adler, who discovered the missing
chapters).

SS, see (iii) above.

Steph. Thes.=Stephani *Thesaurus Graecae Linguae* (Didot).

Sym.=Symmachus's version of O.T.

Targ. (by itself) is used where only one Targum is extant on the
passage quoted.

Targ. Jer., Targ. Jon., and Targ. Onk., see Jer. Targ., Jon. Targ., and
Onk., above.

Tehillim=Midrash on Psalms, ed. Wünsche (2 vols.).

Test. XII Patr.=Testaments of the Twelve Patriarchs ed. Charles,
1908 (Gk., Clarendon Press, Eng., A. & C. Black).

Theod.=Theodotion's version of O.T.

Thes.=Payne Smith's *Thesaurus Syriacus*, Oxf. 1901.

Tromm.=Trommius' *Concordance to the Septuagint.*

Tryph.=the Dialogue between Justin Martyr and Trypho the Jew.

Walton=*Biblia Sacra Polyglotta*, 1657.

Wetst.=Wetstein's *Comm. on the New Testament*, Amsterdam, 1751.

W.H.=Westcott and Hort's New Testament.

Wü.=Wünsche's translation of *Rabboth* etc., 1880—1909 (including
Mechilta, Pesikta Rab Kahana, Tehillim &c.).

(*a*) A bracketed Arabic number, following Mk, Mt., etc., indicates
the number of instances in which a word occurs in Mark, Matthew, etc.,
e.g. ἀγάπη Mk (0), Mt. (1), Lk. (1), Jn (7).

(*b*) Where verses in Hebrew, Greek, and Revised Version, are
numbered differently, the number of R.V. is given alone.

(*c*) In transliterating a Hebrew, Aramaic, or Syriac word, preference
has often, but not invariably, been given to that form which best reveals
the connection between the word in question and forms of it familiar to
English readers. Where a word is not transliterated, it is often indicated
(for the sake of experts) by a reference to Gesen., *Thes.*, Levy, or Levy *Ch.*

CHAPTER I

THE OBJECT OF THIS TREATISE

§ I. "*Fourfold Gospel*" *implies four witnesses*

ALTHOUGH this treatise is not a Harmony of the Gospels, its object may be best explained by reference to the most ancient of such Harmonies, that of Tatian. Tatian, in the second century, broke up and intermixed the four gospels so as to make one continuous and readable gospel "out of," or "through," the "four." In Greek, "through" is *dia*, and "four" is *tessaron*. Hence the name of the Harmony, Diatessaron.

"Through Four" did not mean that all the new biography was attested by all the four biographers. Some parts of the Diatessaron, for example, the Raising of Lazarus, are attested only "through one." Others are attested only "through two," as, for example, the Lord's Prayer through Matthew and Luke, and the Feeding of the Four Thousand through Matthew and Mark. Others, belonging to the Synoptic[1]

---

[1] "Synoptic," applied to the first three gospels, was probably intended to mean that their contents can be, for the most part, "seen together," or "seen at the same time." For example, the descent of the Holy Spirit on Jesus is described by Mark, Matthew, and Luke, in such a way that the accounts can be arranged in three parallel columns and "seen together." But John, though he represents the Baptist as referring to it, does not describe it in such a way as to make a fourth parallel column capable of being "seen together" with the three.

On the quotation of Scripture by the name of the alleged author, *e.g.* Samuel, see References (ii) on p. xiii above.

Tradition—including the great mass of what is common to Matthew, Mark, and Luke—are attested "through three." Only a very few sections of the combined biography—such as the Feeding of the Five Thousand, the Entry into Jerusalem, the Crucifixion, and a word or two uttered by John the Baptist—contain narratives or discourses that can be strictly and exactly described as *attested "through four."*

Now it is only with the things that are *in some sense attested "through four"* that the present work concerns itself. Their special importance is obvious and needs no comment. But some explanation is needed of the reasons for including, among the things "attested through four," passages in which one or more of the four witnesses attests indirectly or even— paradoxical though it may seem—by *verbal omission.*

§ 2. *Luke, sometimes a silent witness*

The following is a good instance of parallelism combined with "*verbal omission.*" In that part of the Fourfold Gospel which records the predictions of the Baptist about his successor, the three columns containing the parallel Matthew, Mark, and Luke, agree in three statements :—(1) He is to be a "mightier one," (2) He is to "baptize with the Holy Spirit," (3) He is to "come." But (4) Matthew and Mark say "come *after me.*" Luke omits "*after me.*"

Our fourth witness, John, differs very widely indeed from the three as to the rest of the words of the Baptist. But as to this particular clause, "*after me,*" he not only inserts it but also repeats it three times. In two of these instances he introduces it in an antithesis with "*before me,*" shewing that "after me," like "before me," may refer to precedence, or may refer to time, or may refer to both. His reiteration gives the impression of an attempt to constrain us to perceive that both the antithetical phrases may have some meaning that lies beneath the surface.

Now are we to exclude all this from our examination of the Fourfold Gospel, on the ground that *"after me"* is attested by only three Evangelists? Surely such an exclusion would be a pedant's error. Common sense seems to dictate inclusion, on the ground that *Luke's reticence may be equivalent*—and, if he is the latest of the three Synoptists, probably is equivalent—*to a kind of tacit testimony*, of the following nature:—

"I do not like this use of *after*. The word used by Matthew and Mark more naturally means *behind*, as though Jesus 'came *behind*' in the character of an attendant. When I come to write about this, in the Acts, writing on my own responsibility, I will take care to use a different word, which shall clearly shew what *after* means[1]. But here I do not like to seem to be correcting, on trivial grounds, a phrase of the ancient Evangelists. So I will simply leave it out."

We do not at present affirm—though we shall do so later on in view of further evidence—that this is what Luke actually meant. But we do affirm already that this is what he may very reasonably and honestly have meant, and that it will be quite reasonable, as well as highly convenient for our purpose, to treat him as one of our four witnesses though only a silent one. Why he was silent, in this and other similar cases, must form part of our future investigations.

As for the Evangelist whom we call "John," he may be regarded as saying, "The temporal and temporary '*behind me*' representing Christ's discipleship, is compatible with a '*before me*' that represents not only Christ's spiritual precedence but also His eternal pre-existence. Instead of omitting '*behind me*,' it will be better to explain it, or better still, not for me to explain it, but to let the Baptist explain to the reader, that he, the Prophet, always understood the '*behind me*' to be merged in a '*before me*'."

[1] See *Son of Man* 3519 *a*, quoting Acts xiii. 25.

We do not at present affirm that this is what John actually meant. But we do affirm already that this is what he may be reasonably supposed to have meant; and we propose, later on, to return to the passage, equipped with further cumulative evidence, and to say "This is what John *did* mean."

§ 3. *John, sometimes an indirect or corrective witness*

One more instance will be given, in which our principle of inclusion will be carried to its extreme limit. It occurs in the accounts of Christ's visit to what Matthew and Mark call "his country," but Luke "Nazareth." Mark's account will be placed first, for reasons that will be given later on[1] :—

Mark, "And *he was not able to do there any mighty work*, save that on a few sick folk he laid his hands and cured them ; and he marvelled because of their unbelief."

Matthew, "And *he did not there many mighty works* because of their unbelief."

Luke omits the sentence.

This Marcan passage has been selected because it is printed by the author of Horae Synopticae[2] as one of several in which the other Synoptists separate themselves from Mark. It is placed under the heading "Passages seeming to limit the power of Jesus Christ." The author shews that, in another passage, a Marcan "*was not able*," when applied to Christ, is avoided by Matthew, and again, in another, by Luke. The Horae makes no reference here to John, whose gospel, for the most part, lies outside its purlieu. But the heading, "Passages seeming to limit...," suggests an inquiry

---

[1] Mk vi. 5—6, Mt. xiii. 58, Lk. iv. 24 foll. (om.). It is open to doubt whether Luke intended to identify the visit he describes with the one described by Mark and Matthew. But the Diatessaron identifies them.

[2] *Horae Synopticae*, by the Rev. Sir John C. Hawkins, Bart., M.A. D.D., 2nd ed. p. 118 (Oxford, 1909). It compares also Mk i. 45 and vii. 24 with the parallel Lk. v. 16 and Mt. xv. 21.

whether John ever similarly "seems to limit." Does he ever venture to say about Christ that He "*was not able to do*" *this or that*? More particularly *does he ever venture to say this in connection with acts of healing*?

The answer is in the affirmative. Not indeed that John describes any visit to Nazareth or performance, or non-performance, of acts of healing there. But he describes an act of healing on the sabbath in Jerusalem, after which Jesus says, "The Son *is able to do nothing of himself* but what he seeth the Father doing[1]."

We do not say that in writing these words John had directly in view the particular passage of Mark above quoted. But we do maintain that the whole question of the Lord's ability to heal, and of His reasons for healing this person and not healing that one, must have confronted Christians in very early times, and must have been brought to a head in this Marcan bluntness of statement, compared with Matthew's smoother version and Luke's silence.

In such cases—especially if we find, as we proceed, many other passages where Mark raises difficult questions that would call for answers in the earliest days of the Church—we ought to attempt to put ourselves in the place of the latest of the Evangelists, and to try to imagine antecedently how he might supply answers to them, while at the same time closely examining his gospel in order to ascertain to what extent, consciously or unconsciously, he has actually supplied them.

Looking, in the first place, from the historical point of view at this question of Christ's ability or inability to heal, we may be sure of this at least, that He never publicly failed. Had He made a single public failure, it is impossible to doubt that the Pharisees would speedily have heard of and

---

[1] Jn v. 19 (lit.) "unless he be [at the moment] seeing the Father doing something." See *Johannine Grammar* 2516, and *Johannine Vocabulary* 1607, quoting Philo i. 414 concerning "the Eldest Son" whom Philo describes as "looking towards" the Father's "archetypal patterns."

utilised it; and their consequent attack on Jesus would have left some trace (in the way of denial, or explanation, or defence) in some passage or other, in some one at least, of our four gospels. But there is no such passage. As to the disciples, the Synoptists do relate that on one occasion they failed in an attempt to cast out an evil spirit; but as to Jesus they all testify that His enemies accused Him not of failure, but of diabolical success, healing with the aid of the devil. The Talmudic evidence, scanty though it is, tends in the same direction[1].

Accepting this, let us now look at the matter from the point of view of the Fourth Evangelist, if we may suppose him to be reviewing all the facts and seeking for an explanation of them. Jesus did not attempt to heal all that came to Him, but, if He attempted, He never failed. Why? Because He always chose the right cases? If so, on what principle did He choose? Was it because He saw something in the patient —faith, for example? Or was it because He felt something in Himself—compassion, for example? Or was it a mixture of these feelings with this insight? Or was it because of something else beyond all these causes?

Does it not seem as though John, in his concrete and dramatic fashion, gives us an answer to these questions—or at all events what he thought an answer—through the story of the healing at the pool of Bethesda? Round that pool lie crowds of sick folk. Jesus selects one. Was it because of the man's faith? The man—a sluggish and unsatisfactory creature, who needs first to be stimulated with a "Dost thou desire to be healed?" and afterwards to be warned with a "No longer continue-sinning, lest a worse thing befall thee" —did not know Jesus by name and person even when he had been healed[2], and therefore can hardly be said to have had

---

[1] See *Christianity in Talmud and Midrash*, R. T. Herford, pp. 103 foll., 108 foll., on "Healing in the name of Jesus."

[2] Jn v. 13 "He that was healed knew not who it was...."

"faith" in Jesus as Jesus, that is to say, as the well-known "Jesus of Nazareth, the Exorcist, and Healer." Was it then any foreknowledge possessed by Jesus of the man's ultimate reform? It is not so said. And, against it, is the fact that the man, after receiving this warning, actually goes and informs "the Jews" of the name of his benefactor, whom they consequently "persecute." Was it then simply the Lord's compassion for the man's long-continued disease? That is indeed suggested by the statement that Jesus "knew that he had been a long time" thus. But it is no more than suggested. And what about the rest—the "multitude of the sick, blind, halt, withered"? If "compassion" is to be considered as the motive, had Christ no crumbs of "compassion" to cast to one or two of them?

The conclusion to which John seems to desire to lead us is, that when Jesus healed on earth, it was because He saw an act of healing ordained for Him from heaven. When He did not heal—and there were multitudes of such cases—it was not because He did not pity, but because He did not "see" the act revealed to Him from heaven as His appointed "work." This, of course, does not explain anything to us unless we believe that Jesus had special promptings from the Father in heaven which controlled the general impulse of compassion. But, if we believe this, we can understand how Jesus may have passed through multitudes of sick and suffering people, pitying yet not healing, as Elijah passed by many widows in Israel till he came, under the guidance of God, to the widow of Sarepta[1].

"In such cases," John seems to say, "the Son, being in a divine unity with the Father, '*was not able*,' as Mark says, '*to perform any mighty-work*.' Mark calls it 'a *mighty-work*.' Matthew and Luke use the same term when describing the Lord's acts of healing. But I prefer to call them '*signs*.'

---

[1] Lk. iv. 26.

7

For they were '*signs*' of the Father's will. Called by that name, the acts indicate that they could not occur on earth if they had not counterparts, or what Philo calls 'patterns[1],' in heaven. Mark was justified in saying that at Nazareth Jesus *was not able to do any mighty work*; but the reason was that He *was not able to do anything against the will of God*, which always guided His actions."

The arguments for the inclusion of this Marcan tradition and its Johannine equivalent will apply, *mutatis mutandis*, to many other traditions peculiar to Mark, *or to Mark and Matthew*. The reasons for not adding "*or to Mark and Luke*," will appear fully as we go on. Here it may be said briefly that where Luke agrees with Mark, John, as a rule, does *not* intervene. The reasons for placing Mark first will be stated in the next Chapter.

---

[1] See p. 5, n. 1.

CHAPTER II

WHICH GOSPEL SHOULD STAND FIRST?

§ 1. *The need of some fixed order*

ON the answer to the question that forms the heading of this Chapter the arrangement of our whole work depends. This will be best seen from the first passage quoted in Chapter I, where John the Baptist uses about Jesus the words "cometh *after me.*" Finding the phrase "*after me*" omitted by Luke alone, we there treated Luke as omitting what was in his predecessors, Matthew and Mark, and John as (so to speak) rehabilitating it by explanation. Thus we seemed tacitly to adopt the common order—Matthew, Mark, Luke, John.

But in the second passage, where we quoted Mark as saying that Jesus "*was not able* to do there any mighty work," we placed Mark first; Matthew second, as omitting the italicised words; Luke third, as omitting the whole of the sentence; John fourth, as applying the phrase elsewhere to Jesus in an explanatory context.

The time has now come to decide on some order in which to discuss the variations of the four Evangelists. If the four gospels had been written independently about the same time, it might have been difficult to come to any general and logical decision. In order to preserve impartiality we might have found it necessary to lay down no fixed rule but to give the first place now to one gospel, now to another. Or we might have taken the briefest account first, as being likely to be the oldest, and

9

the longer accounts afterwards, as being likely to be later amplifications. Or we might have taken the longest account first, as being perhaps in some cases the earliest, and the shorter ones afterwards, as being condensations. Either of these courses would have introduced inconvenient complexities. From these we shall be saved if we can prove that one of the Synoptists should stand before the other two; for it will not be difficult to shew that the three Synoptists preceded John.

§ 2. *Mark should stand first*

The detailed demonstration of the priority of Mark—for it is a demonstration and not a mere establishment of a probability—may be found elsewhere[1]. But the outline of it can be given here in a form intelligible to the general reader, and sufficiently full for our present purpose. That purpose is to shew that the great body of what is called the Synoptic narrative in Mark is older than the corresponding narratives in Matthew and Luke[2]. The reader must note the words "great body." We do not deny that Mark, like other gospels, may include traditions varying in date as well as in the degree of their authenticity or accuracy; but we assert that Mark contains a great mass of narrative which must be earlier than the corresponding narratives in Matthew and Luke, because it can be shewn that Matthew and Luke have independently borrowed from it.

This the reader can verify for himself as follows. Let him take some Synoptic passage in which the three Synoptists shew considerable agreement, and place their texts in three parallel columns, writing the parts that are common to *all*

---

[1] See *Corrections of Mark* **314—30**, and the Preface to Rushbrooke's *Synopticon*.

[2] The reader should note that the Synoptic narrative has nothing to do with what might be called the Matthew-Luke record containing the longer discourses of the Lord. See the definition of Synoptic above, p. I, n. I.

three in red. Then let him underline the parts common
(1) to *Mark and Matthew alone* with one line, (2) to *Mark
and Luke alone* with two lines, (3) to *Matthew and Luke
alone* with three lines[1]. He will find that the red portion,
though it may not be copious, is generally sufficient to indicate
the drift of the discourse or narrative. For the rest, (1) the
one-lined portion will often contain much, especially toward
the end of the gospel. (2) The two-lined portion also will
often contain much, especially toward the beginning of the
gospel. But (3) *the three-lined portion will contain often
nothing at all, and rarely or never anything of great doctrinal
importance*[2].

Why is the three-lined, that is, the Matthew-Luke portion,
so insignificant? Why do we not find Matthew occasionally
agreeing with Luke alone, or Luke with Matthew alone[3]?
Why do we always find that Matthew, when he agrees with
Luke, *agrees with Mark as well*; and that Luke, when he
agrees with Matthew, *agrees with Mark as well*? It is because
Matthew and Luke are in the position of two schoolboys,
Primus and Tertius, seated on the same form, between whom
sits another, Secundus (Mark). All three are writing (we will
suppose) a narrative of the same event, or a translation of the
same passage of a classical author. Primus and Tertius

---

[1] This is done in Rushbrooke's *Synopticon* (Macmillan), pp. vi—vii
where the triple tradition is printed in red, and the purpose of the under-
lining is effected by variations of type.

[2] It consists of little more than such grammatical or slight verbal
alterations of Mark's text as might be expected in some edition of Mark
(a little later than ours) from which Matthew and Luke borrowed. See
Diatessarica Part II, which deals with what are there called "The
Corrections of Mark Adopted by Matthew and Luke," and with inferences
that may be derived from them.

[3] We do find Luke agreeing with Matthew alone occasionally in
short insertions such as the doctrine of baptizing with fire. But this
(Mt. iii. 11, Lk. iii. 16) is quite outside Mark (i. 8) who only speaks of
baptizing with the Spirit. Both the style and the subject-matter indicate
that the insertion belongs to the separate tradition of Matthew and Luke.

copy largely from Secundus. Occasionally the two copy the same words; then we have the red stream, indicating the agreement of three writers. At other times Primus (Matthew) copies what Tertius (Luke) does not; then we have the one-lined stream (Mark-Matthew). At others, Tertius (Luke) copies what Primus (Matthew) does not; then we have the two-lined (Mark-Luke). But Primus and Tertius *cannot look over one another's shoulders. Hence a three-lined stream, of any importance for doctrinal purposes, is non-existent*[1].

It is tempting to pass on at once to a similar question about Quartus, that is to say, John: "From whom, if from any of the three, does he, the last of the four Evangelists, borrow?" But we have not yet proved that John *is* "the last of the four Evangelists." It will be best to discuss that subject in the next Chapter, and meanwhile to content ourselves with the conclusion that Mark must be placed before Matthew and Luke because they have independently borrowed from him in those portions of their gospels to which Mark is parallel.

---

[1] See *Corrections of Mark* **314—30**. The object of that treatise is to shew that the few and unimportant similarities of Matthew and Luke in the Synoptic Tradition, where there is a parallel Mark—which contrast conspicuously with the many and important close similarities of Matthew and Luke in the Double Tradition, or Tradition of Doctrine, where there is no parallel Mark—are probably to be explained by the fact that Matthew and Luke in many cases borrowed from the same corrected edition of Mark.

CHAPTER III

WHICH GOSPEL SHOULD STAND LAST?

§ 1. *Internal evidence*

THAT John should be placed after the Synoptists may be made almost certain by the internal evidence of his subject-matter and by the language in which he expresses it.

It can be shewn that, in some cases, while omitting Synoptic narrative, he expressly assumes that his readers know it, and that, in other cases, he must have made this assumption although he does not express it. For example, take the following Synoptic events, 1st, the baptism of Jesus by the Baptist, 2nd, the descent of the Holy Spirit, 3rd, the Baptist's imprisonment by Herod. About the first he is silent, but we know that he must have assumed it from what is in the context. As for the second, he represents the Baptist as expressly saying, before it happens, " Upon whomsoever *thou shalt see the Spirit descending and abiding upon him.*" As for the third, he expressly says, " *John was not yet cast into prison,*" without telling us when, or why, or by whom, the prophet was imprisoned. Obviously he assumes all the three facts to be so well known that no one will be perplexed by his silence about the first and by the brevity of his allusions to the second and the third. All three might justly be regarded as essential to any treatise that professed to be an early biography of Jesus; but they might be omitted in a supplement to early biographies.

The same argument applies to much other Synoptic matter, as for example, the Institution of the Lord's Supper. The omission of it indicates, *inter alia*, that it was too well known to require attestation of the simple fact (whatever variations there might be as to details).

So much for the subject-matter. In the next place comes the evidence from the language. This has been fully discussed in one of the parts of Diatessarica entitled Johannine Vocabulary, where it is shewn that John systematically and deliberately chooses different words from those of the Synoptists, so that, for example, he never uses the nouns "faith" or "repentance."

Some one may say, "But might not this be the sign of the earliest, not of the latest, of the Evangelists? What if John, coming first, represents Christ's language exactly, while the Synoptists, coming afterwards, represent it inexactly?" The answer is, "That is impossible for the following reason. John represents Jesus as speaking in precisely the same style and words as he himself uses when he is writing about Jesus, or as the Baptist uses when he is speaking about Jesus. The style and the vocabulary are so uniform that commentators on the Fourth Gospel, from the earliest times, have been divided, and still are divided, as to where the words of Jesus sometimes end and the words of the Evangelist begin."

The deliberateness with which John regularly diverged from the Synoptic vocabulary may be illustrated by one instance in particular, his habit of assigning to Jesus, in place of the Synoptists' simple "*verily*," a twofold "*verily, verily.*" In a gospel that abounds in mystical or poetical repetitions, such a repetition may possibly have a mystical meaning; but in any case the divergence from the Synoptic language is very remarkable and must be deliberate[1].

---

[1] See *Johannine Grammar* **2611** *a* "It may be illustrated by the surprise that would have been felt by readers of Boswell's biography

§2. *External evidence that John "supplied things omitted"*

Very ancient external evidence testifies, not only to the posteriority of John, but also to his attitude toward the Synoptists, as a supplier of "things omitted" by them. Eusebius justifies the reasonableness of "the ancients" in "cataloguing" his gospel as "a fourth part to the other three," and gives the ancient view in the words of the ancients themselves.

It comes very nearly to this, that the Fourth Gospel was, in one respect, related to the Three as the Book of Chronicles was related to the Books of Samuel and Kings[1]. In the LXX, the Book of Chronicles is entitled *Paraleipomena*, "Things Passed Over," or, "Things Omitted," that is to say, things omitted in Kings and added (as a supplement to Kings) in Chronicles. Somewhat similarly it was supposed by "the ancients" that John supplemented the Synoptists. "The ancients" did not indeed mention Kings and Chronicles. Had they done so, they would doubtless have recognised that the tone and the spirit of the Evangelist were very different from the tone and the spirit of the Chronicler. But they said that the Evangelist supplemented the earlier gospels. And the title of Chronicles in the LXX implies that the Chronicler supplemented Kings.

It will be best to give the ancient tradition in its own words : "John had been all the time confining himself to oral preaching, when he was finally induced to write for the following reason. When the circulation of the three previously written [gospels] had brought them at last to him [*i.e.* John],

coming upon a new life of Dr Johnson in which '*Sir, Sir*' was regularly substituted for '*Sir*'." The uniformity of style is all the more remarkable because of the individuality of the *dramatis personae*, John the Baptist, Nicodemus, the Samaritan Woman, Peter, Philip, &c.

[1] For brevity, in the following passages comparing "Chronicles" with "Samuel and Kings," the latter will be shortened into "Kings." The LXX regards them as four "Books of the Kings."

as also to everyone, he accepted them indeed and testified to their truth; but [added] that the only thing left out in the writing [of the three] was the account of Christ's acts at first, and at the beginning of the preaching [of the gospel]."

Here Eusebius parenthetically justifies this view by pointing out that Mark and Matthew expressly define the beginning of Christ's preaching of the gospel—and that Luke somewhat similarly implies the beginning—as *not occurring till after the arrest of the Baptist*. Then Eusebius resumes the tradition of "the ancients."

It declared that for these reasons John, by request, recorded in his gospel what the Synoptists had passed over, and especially the events before the Baptist's imprisonment. John himself (so the tradition maintained) attested this very view. First, at one time, he said "This beginning of his wonderful works did Jesus"; secondly, at another time, he mentioned the Baptist, in the midst of the acts of Jesus, as still baptizing at Aenon; and he made the matter absolutely clear in the following sentence "For John was not yet cast into prison[1]."

Eusebius adds that, since Matthew and Luke had previously given the Saviour's genealogy according to the flesh, it ought to seem natural that John passed it over in silence and began from the divine origin of the Logos or Word[2].

---

[1] Jn ii. 11, iii. 23—4.
[2] Euseb. iii. 24. 7—13. Comp. *ib.* vi. 14. 5 foll., where τῶν εὐαγγελίων τὰ περιέχοντα τὰς γ. should probably not be rendered "*of the gospels, those that contain the genealogies* were written first," but "*of the gospels, those [parts] that contain as their substance* (or, *have as their contents*) (or, *consist of copies of*) *the genealogies* were written first." See instances in *Enc. Bibl.* "Gospels" col. 1823, to which add Joseph. *Ant.* xii. 4. 10, 11, where (Whiston) "the copy whereof here follows" and "these were the contents (τοῦτον περιεῖχε τὸν τρόπον)" are used about the same epistle. The phrase recurs in *ib.* xiii. 4. 9, &c. It was natural that genealogies should be, or at all events should be supposed to be, committed to writing at an early date.

Later on in his history, Eusebius quotes from Clement of Alexandria a very early statement—as made by "the elders from the beginning"—not only attesting the early date of the genealogies but also declaring that John, last of the four Evangelists, "seeing-in-a-general-view that (lit.) the things according to the body were indicated in the [existing] gospels, composed a spiritual gospel at the urgent request of the disciples, and under the divine impulse of the Spirit[1]."

§ 3. *John should stand last*

The words of Clement just quoted should guard us against a modern danger. It is hard for us, Gentiles of the twentieth century, to realise that a Jewish evangelist—or at all events such a one as the unknown author of the Fourth Gospel whom we call John—might be at one and the same time influenced by details in written gospels and yet "moved by divine impulse." But if we are to do justice to the Clementine tradition, we must endeavour to put ourselves in the position of a Christian teacher at the end of the first century, imbued with the Spirit of the Son of God, and receiving somewhat late—so the tradition implies—three widely differing documents about Him, which had been gradually growing into an authoritative circulation. One of these (Mark) spoke of a "beginning" without any genealogy of the Saviour. Another (Matthew) traced His genealogical descent from Abraham through a "*Joseph*" *begotten by* "*Jacob.*" A third (Luke) traced a different genealogical descent. It went up to Abraham indeed, but also to Adam. And it went up—with a modifying clause, "as was supposed"—through a "*Joseph*

---

[1] Euseb. vi. 14. 5—7. In this context, "the things-according-to-the-body" probably alludes to the genealogies in particular, as describing descent after the flesh, but does not exclude a more general meaning. On "the disciples (τῶν γνωρίμων)" see Mayor's note on Clem. Alex. 863—4. But it may mean "friends." It will be seen later on that Jerome seems to take it as "brethren."

the son of Heli." There were also many other points of
difference between the two genealogies[1].

Some converts might well be perplexed, others might be
divided into conflicting parties, by discrepancies of this kind
(however explained). In their perplexities and controversies,
too many might ignore, for the time, that spiritual descent
of the Son on earth from the Father in heaven which would
seem to the author of the Fourth Gospel to outweigh altogether
the importance of these genealogies after the flesh. Let us
also add some thought of the minor but not slight pain that
would be felt by such a writer—whose identity we do not
know but whom we must feel to be honestly and earnestly
writing in the name of "the disciple whom Jesus loved"—at
the occasion thereby given to the enemies of the Church for
stopping the present influx of new converts, and for holding
up the preachers of the Truth to lasting ridicule and reprobation, as preaching what was demonstrated by the preachers
themselves to be flagrantly inconsistent and false.

Bringing ourselves face to face with these facts, we shall
be better able to see that there is much more antecedent
probability than we might have supposed in Clement's view,
and that the beginnings of the Three Gospels—not excluding
that of Mark—may have been for days and nights in the
mind of the writer of the prologue of the Fourth Gospel
before he was inspired to utter its opening words. Such an
inspiration as is imputed to him by the Clementine tradition,

---

[1] *E.g.*, the son of David from whom Luke (iii. 31) traces the Messiah's
descent is not, as in Mt. i. 6, "Solomon," whom "David begat of her
[that had been the wife] of Uriah," but Nathan. The author of Luke's
genealogy might very well believe that Nathan—placed before Solomon
in 2 S. v. 14, and presumably older than Solomon—was not the son of
Bathsheba, whose eldest surviving son (2 S. xii. 24) appears to have been
Solomon. Schöttgen (on Lk. iii. 31) quotes a tradition from *Sohar* that
Hephzibah (Is. lxii. 4) "*the wife of Nathan the son of David*" is "*the
mother of the Messiah.*"

This avoids what some—in spite of Jerome (on Mt. i. 3—6)—might
regard as a stumbling-block.

so far from being inconsistent, is admirably accordant, with the supposition that he was also influenced, or even constrained, by the entreaties of those who saw the dangers impending on the Church from "genealogies" of all sorts, arising as rivals to the genealogies in Matthew and Luke. Jerome expressly says that John was thus "compelled by the brethren," but goes on to speak of him as also inspired: "At last," he says, "saturated with revelation, John burst out with that proem, coming from heaven, '*In the beginning was the Word, and the Word was with God and the Word was God*[1].'"

This is excellently said. But when will Christians begin to recognise its excellence? How long will it be before they perceive that it was possible in the first century for one and the same Christian to see visions and receive revelations from the Lord and even to be snatched up into the third heaven to hear words of glory, and yet to give a Roman Governor the impression of being a crazy pedant, "Thou art mad, Paul. Thy much book-learning doth turn thee to madness"?

But to return to the question of chronological order. The consensus of external and internal evidence makes it practically certain that John's gospel should be placed chronologically last. It also revives the interesting question that has already come before us, "Does John—on those occasions on which he intervenes in Synoptic tradition—favour the earliest of the Synoptists (Mark), or one of the two later Synoptists (Matthew or Luke)?" The answer must be reserved for the next Chapter. For the present we are content to say that, as Mark is the earliest of the Four Evangelists, in that portion of the biography of Christ which contains the Synoptic Tradition, so John is the latest.

---

[1] Jerome, *Pref. to Comm. on Matthew*: "Unde et ecclesiastica narrat historia, cum a fratribus cogeretur ut scriberet, ita facturum se respondisse, si indicto jejunio in commune omnes Deum deprecarentur, quo expleto, revelatione saturatus, illud prooemium e caelo veniens eructavit...." There is perhaps a play of words on "jejunio" and "saturatus." A similar tradition is recorded in the Muratorian Tablet, see *Enc. Bibl.*, col. 1821—2.

CHAPTER IV

ALLUSIONS IN JOHN TO MARK

§ 1. *The naturalness of such allusions*

THE certainty that Matthew and Luke borrowed from Mark makes it probable that John also, when supplementing the Three Gospels, would have Mark specially in view. Not indeed that he would often borrow from Mark's language where he agreed with Mark, or contradict Mark's language where he disagreed from Mark; for, as we have seen above, John deliberately deviates from Synoptic language. But we might expect him occasionally to intervene, using Johannine language, in some passages where Mark was misleading, or obscure, or so harsh in expression as to give unnecessary offence, and where Matthew and Luke had either contented themselves with omitting the Marcan expression or had explained it in a manner that might not seem to go quite to the root of some latent spiritual truth.

§ 2. *An impartial collection of groups of Marcan peculiarities*

In order to test this hypothesis of Johannine allusion to Mark we need an impartial collection of Marcan peculiarities of the kind just described—passages for various reasons likely to be omitted by later evangelists and actually omitted by Matthew and Luke. It should be impartial, because the collector ought not to be biassed by any theory of Johannine allusion to Mark. Moreover, we ought to have, if they could be collected, similar collections of repellent passages in Matthew and Luke, that we might examine John's attitude to them also. For such impartial collections we naturally turn to the section entitled "Statistics and Observations" on Mark, Matthew and Luke, in Horae Synopticae, illustrating with detailed quotations or references the peculiarities of the several Synoptists. This section gives various groups of Marcan peculiarities to which we find nothing corresponding under "Matthew" and "Luke." First come "Passages seeming (*a*) to limit the power of Jesus Christ, or (*b*) to be otherwise derogatory to, or unworthy of, Him." Of the former there are seven instances; of the latter, fifteen. Next come "Passages seeming to disparage the attainments or character of the Apostles." Of these there are seven. Then come "Other passages which might cause offence or difficulty," of which there are seventeen. The total is forty-six.

Now according to a strict and literal interpretation of the title "fourfold gospel" we should be excluded from dealing with any of these forty-six instances. For, even if John alluded to them, the result would be, literally speaking, no more than a "twofold gospel." But in the first group of these instances we find that Marcan passage quoted in our first Chapter—one that appeared well worth including in our investigation, if we wished to include parallelism of evangelic thoughts as well as words—saying that "Jesus *was not able* to do any mighty work."

Continuing, then, to adhere to the principle of inclusiveness there laid down, let us make the following experiment, in which no one will be able to say that we evolved a theory first, and then selected such instances only as were favourable to us afterwards. Let us take the first group of seven instances given in the Horae Synopticae and ask, in each case, "Has John anything to say about this?" If he intervenes in favour of Mark, we shall not expect close similarity of expression. On the contrary, we shall expect dissimilarity, because we know by this time that John systematically avoids Synoptic language. It will be enough for us if John is shewn to intervene in behalf of the *thought* in Mark. But of course any discovery that he intervenes in *word* as well as thought will have additional weight in inclining the balance toward the conclusion that when Mark is departed from by Matthew and Luke, John intervenes.

If John does not intervene, then we shall admit that, so far, our theory fails.

§ 3. *Johannine allusions to some of these*

Of the seven instances (*a*) above mentioned as being grouped together in Horae Synopticae two refer to healing by means of "spittle." In the Talmud, R. Jochanan is said to have declared that "whispering" over a wound to heal it, when accompanied with "spitting," deprived a man of eternal life, since the name of God ought not to be pronounced after spitting[1]. And it is easy to understand that for other reasons, including a suggestion of unseemliness, such a detail may have "given offence" to readers whom the later evangelists kept in view. The soaring mysticism of the Fourth Gospel— which nowhere mentions such words as leper, unclean, or even hypocrisy—makes the appearance of such a detail there quite unexpected. Yet there it appears. Moreover it is in a context that emphasizes the fact and probably connects it with a mystical suggestion[2].

One of the two Marcan instances of healing with "spittle"

---

[1] Levy iv. 470 *b* quoting *Sanhedr.* 101 *a*.

[2] Jn ix. 6—7 "When he had thus spoken, he spat on the ground, and made clay of the *spittle*, and anointed his eyes with the clay, and said unto him, Go, wash in the pool of Siloam (which is, by interpretation, Sent)." The blind man is the Gentile world, born again. In the new-born proselyte, the old eye must be closed before the new one is opened, see Levy iv. 154 *b* quoting *Lev. r.* (on Lev. xii. 2).

describes the cure of a blind man, effected not at once but as it were in two stages. The Johannine instance of the cure of a man born blind and healed by "spittle" is of a similar description, as being effected by two acts, though not, as in Mark, first partially and then completely[1]. No such instances either of partial followed by complete cure, or of cure performed in two stages, are recorded by Matthew or Luke.

Horae Synopticae adds in a note that "perhaps painful effort might seem to be implied" in the Marcan words "Looking up to heaven, *he sighed*," and contrasts the Marcan "*sighing deeply in his spirit*" with the parallel Matthew which omits this detail[2]. With these peculiarities of Mark we may compare peculiarities of John describing Jesus as (R.V.) "*groaning in the spirit*," and (R.V.) "*groaning in himself*," just before He "lifted up his eyes" and pronounced the appeal to the Father which precedes the raising of Lazarus from the dead[3].

Another instance in the Horae—also referring to healing—was touched on above in our first Chapter, and John was there shewn to be apparently justifying a Marcan statement that, in certain circumstances, Jesus "*was not able* to do any mighty work," by words of Jesus Himself, "The Son *is able to do nothing* of himself." Here it may be added that "*not able*" is applied elsewhere to Christ by Matthew, as well as Mark. But it is from the lips of His enemies, "He saved others; *he is not able to save himself*." There, again, Luke omits "*not able*."

In view of all these facts we naturally ask whether there is any Johannine instance (like that of Matthew) in which Christ's enemies, whether secret or open, say about Him—and especially about Him as Healer or Lifegiver—"*he was not able*." According to ordinary interpretation there is none.

---

[1] Mk viii. 22—6 (a blind man), Jn ix. 1—7 (a man blind from birth).

[2] Mk vii. 34, and Mk viii. 12 parall. to Mt. xvi. 2.

[3] Jn xi. 33, 38, 41. See also R.V. margin.

But take the following comment about Christ's being "*not able*" to do what He wished, which John puts into the mouth of "*some*" of "*the Jews*," near the grave of Lazarus: "The Jews therefore said, See, how he loved him! *But some of them said*, This man, who opened the eyes of the blind [man], *was not able* to prevent this man [Lazarus] also from dying!" The Revised Version renders this interrogatively, "Was not this man able?" But there are no grounds for taking the Greek "*not*" interrogatively in this passage. It is not so taken by the earliest authorities. If the early Latin translators had regarded it as interrogative, they would have rendered it by "nonne" instead of "non," according to their custom. But they render it negatively ("non"). Moreover there is an apparent intention to distinguish, by a "*but*," the kindly Jews, who emphasized Christ's love, from the malignant Jews, who emphasized His (supposed) weakness.

In accordance, then, with grammatical as well as psychological considerations, the words must be taken as an utterance of malignity, "throwing doubt" (as ancient authorities say) on the genuineness of Christ's healing of the man born blind[1]. It would come under the heading in Horae Synopticae as "limiting Christ's power." It creates no difficulty in the Johannine narrative any more than in Mark and Matthew, because the words are uttered by enemies. But the passages, taken together, shew that an evangelist might shrink from using the phrase in his own person, as if he might be supposed to be using it of the Saviour in a hostile sense.

---

[1] See Cramer (on Jn xi. 36—7) where it is said that they "malignantly referred to that miracle as though it had not [really] come to pass." The commentator apparently read the words about opening the eyes of the blind as meaning "who opened [so it is said]." And there is irony in "was not able [strange to say]." The early Syriac Version known as Syro-Sinaitic (SS) inserts a rare word meaning "*forsooth*," implying contempt or surprised incredulity, (lit.) "not forsooth was he (*or*, would he have been) able to make this [one] that he should not die."

We pass to a very different instance. No great principle is involved in it. It is merely that Mark appears to have placed in one narrative about a storm a clause that John transfers to another narrative about a storm. The clause occurs, in Mark, at the beginning of the threefold Synoptic narrative of the storm in which Jesus fell asleep. Mark says that the disciples "take (*or*, receive) him, as he was, in the boat, *and other boats were with him*[1]." Horae Synopticae calls attention to the italicised words, and says "It might be wondered how the 'other boats' weathered the storm. (Perhaps however Mark did not mean to imply that these also crossed the lake.)" The clause about "*other boats*" seems out of place, having no meaning here. Matthew and Luke, besides omitting it, omit also the words "take (*or*, receive) him, as he was, in the boat." It will be shewn in due course, when we discuss this narrative in its order, that John inserts both these clauses (slightly changed) but inserts them elsewhere. There are two storms in the gospels. John, who omits (what Luke retains) the storm in which Jesus fell asleep, but inserts (what Luke omits) the storm in which Jesus walked on the waters, apparently regards the Marcan clause as placed wrongly in the former, its right place being in the latter. At all events a clause about "*other boats*[2]" finds its place in the context following the Johannine account of the latter. There it seems better in place, being connected with the question "How did Jesus come from one side of the Lake to the other?" The clause about "taking (*or*, receiving)[3]" Jesus "in the boat" also finds its fit place there, in the words

---

[1] Mk iv. 36.

[2] Jn vi. 23 (A.V.) "*other boats*." The text has many variations. Some of them are caused by the ambiguity of the Gk unaccented αλλα, which may mean "*others*" or "*but*." SS must be added to the versions that adopt "*other*."

[3] The Greek word, παραλαμβάνω, used by Mk, occurs in Jn i. 11 "his own *received* him not," but it often means "take along with oneself."

" They therefore desired to *take him into the boat*, and straight-way the boat was by the land to which they were going[1]."

Another instance, of quite a different kind from the one just quoted, is the statement of Mark—when describing how Joseph came to beg the body of Jesus—that " Pilate *marvelled if he were already dead*[2]." Horae Synopticae adds " It might have been thought at least needless to introduce this question into ordinary teaching"—presumably meaning that it would lead doubters to say, " And might not Pilate well ' marvel '? *Jesus was not really dead.* He had merely swooned." Hence perhaps the Acta Pilati (B) places Pilate's marvel before, not after, Joseph's entrance, and represents it as being caused by the report of the centurion concerning all the "great miracles " (the " earthquake," " darkness," &c.) that had attended the death of Jesus[3].

John inserts details (not in any of the Synoptists) which negative the supposition of a mere swoon. " Soldiers," he says in effect, " had been sent by Pilate to ensure, by the regular *crurifragium* (i.e. breaking the legs), the death of all those crucified. Jesus had died already, and, to make sure that He was actually dead, one of the soldiers pierced His side with a spear, inflicting a wound whence ' there came out blood and water. And he that hath seen hath borne witness, and his witness is true[4]'." By these details, without trenching on the Synoptic narrative[5], John removes an objection that

---

[1] Jn vi. 21.   [2] Mk xv. 44.   [3] *Acta Pilati* (B) § 11.

[4] Jn xix. 34—5. On the probable symbolism see *Light on the Gospel* **3999** (iii) 13 *a*, and on the following words "and *he* (ἐκεῖνος) knoweth that he (unemph.) saith true," see *Johannine Grammar* **2383—4.**

[5] Reading the text of Mark after that of John, as it is placed in the Diatessaron, we see that Joseph may be supposed to have informed Pilate of the death of Jesus *before the centurion* had reported the death: "Joseph asked the body of Jesus [who, he said, had already died]. But Pilate wondered if he had indeed already died, and he called the centurion to him and questioned him…" John does not mention Pilate's " wonder-ing," but he leaves us able to say, with the aid of the Johannine additions,

ALLUSIONS IN JOHN TO MARK

might have been derived from the earliest of the Synoptists by an opponent of the Christians. And, as in the story of healing by "spittle," he meets it with an explanation that apparently has a mystical interpretation.

"But the explanation may not be true." That, though it will be the main point ultimately, is not the main point at present. We are considering, at present, not the Evangelist's veracity, nor his accuracy, but his method in general, and his allusions to Mark in particular. The reader may feel disposed to say, "These are small matters. They do not help me." But they are not "small," and they ought to "help" him, if they prove that the Evangelist, mystic though he was, and poet though he was, believed himself to be a historian, too, and used every particle that he could find of misunderstood tradition in the oldest of the Gospels, in order to bring out what he conceived to be the historical truth, while at the same time tingeing it with a spiritual and symbolical interpretation.

No serious student of the Christianity of the first century can be ignorant of the probability of the existence of many "gospels," or "gospel-traditions," besides the Three, some written, some unwritten; some of Greek, some of Hebraic, tendency; some in the tone and spirit of prose, some in that of poetry[1]. From the most ancient and most misunderstood of these, John may be inferred to have probably borrowed— *if he can be proved to have borrowed from Mark.* Regarded in this light, the proof of the borrowing from Mark is by no means a "small matter," and may "help" us far on the way toward the historical truth.

In this particular case, it may appear that there are

"Pilate 'wondered' at first, when he heard the news from Joseph, but not afterwards when he heard the whole news."

The historical fact is not discussed above. The point is merely this, that the details added by John are adapted to remove the difficulties raised by Mark.

[1] See p. 38.

grounds for believing that although the vision of the flow of the stream of blood and water from Christ's side was subjective, the *crurifragium* and the piercing of the side were historical facts.

§ 4. *An instance that seems at first sight not worth noticing*

The sixth instance in the Horae Synopticae (placed last of the seven here because of its important bearing on the following Chapters) contains nothing but a detail, peculiar to the Marcan story of the Withering of the Fig-tree, and implying that the tree was not withered instantaneously. Small though this detail is, the examination of it will help us (I think) to understand why Matthew differs from Mark as to other parts of the story, and why Luke omits the whole.

Mark says that it was not till the morning after the tree was cursed that the disciples, "*going by, early*, saw the fig-tree withered from its roots[1]." Matthew writes thus, "He saith unto it, Let there be no fruit from thee henceforward for ever. And *immediately* the fig-tree withered away[2]." Luke, though he omits the story of the Withering of the Fig-tree, has a parable that might be called the Probation of the Fig-tree. In that, the Fig-tree is at first doomed to an immediate fall ("Cut it down") because the Lord of the Orchard has come "three years[3]" to it and found no fruit. Then the Gardener intercedes ("Lord, let it alone this year also") that it may have one last interval of grace. Both the Withering of the Fig-tree and the Probation of the Fig-tree would well apply

---

[1] Mk xi. 20. [2] Mt. xxi. 19.

[3] Concerning the (Lk. xiii. 7) "three years," Schöttgen ii. 548 quotes two traditions (to which add *Pesikt.* Wü. p. 150, n. 4) representing the Shechinah as going out of the City, and "standing three years and a half on the Mount of Olives," and bidding the men of Jerusalem to "repent" (Jer. xiii. 16) "before the darkness falls" upon them. The prediction "three years and a half" is illustrated by Dan. xii. 7 "A time, times, and half a time."

to the barren Church of the Jews[1]. Here, the important question may suggest itself, " Did Luke omit the Marcan miracle because he believed Mark to have misunderstood a parable as fact?" But we must not digress to that. Engaged as we are in an experimental testing of the rule that " where Luke omits or alters Marcan tradition, John often intervenes," we must confine ourselves to this question, " Does John intervene in any way as to the subject of the tree? Directly, literally, and verbally, we know he does not. And we do not expect it. But if we could get to the *thought* underlying the Marcan Withering of the Tree, should we find John intervening indirectly and spiritually? If so, where?

For a full discussion of this question the reader is referred to a previous part of Diatessarica[2]. But the substance of it can be given here so far as concerns an illustration from Jewish metaphor bearing on parallel passages in which Jesus promises the disciples that they shall cast (Mark and Matthew) "this mountain," or (Luke) "this sycamine-tree," into the sea :—

Mk xi. 23	Mt. xxi. 21	Lk. xvii. 6
Whosoever shall say to *this mountain*...	Not only the [deed] of *the fig-tree* shall ye do, but even if ye shall say to *this mountain*...	Ye should be saying to *this* [or, *the*] *sycamine-tree*...

It appears from many quotations that "*this plane-tree*" and "*this mountain*" were terms used contemptuously by the Jews to denote the Samaritan worship on Mount Gerizim, where it was supposed that Jacob had buried "strange gods"

---

[1] Origen, on Mt. xxi. 20 (the Withering of the Fig-tree) combines Lk. xiii. 7 (the Parable of Probation). He does not confuse the two, and of course he does not deny the miracle ; but he recognises that the Marcan miracle and the Lucan parable apply to the same thing, the unfruitful tree of Israel. The Docētae are said by Hippolytus (*Haer.* viii. 1) to have quoted words from the two Traditions in a confused form.

[2] See *Son of Man* 3364 *i—q*, which contains a separate Note on "This Sycamine-tree."

under a "*terebinth tree*" called by various names. A great number of passages describe conversations in which a typical Samaritan suggests to a typical Jewish Rabbi, on his way through Samaria to Jerusalem, that it would be better to stay and worship "*in this plane-tree*" (paraphrased in some English translations as "*in this mountain*").

These facts recall the Johannine Dialogue between Jesus and the Samaritan woman, in which the latter suddenly deviates from the personal question of "five husbands" to the public and national controversy about *this mountain*: "Sir, I perceive that thou art a prophet. Our fathers worshipped in *this mountain*; and ye say that in Jerusalem is the place where men ought to worship."

There are many indications that, in Christ's days, the service of the Temple, and the priestly monopolies connected with it, and the superstitious devotion to the external details of it, went far to convert what the Jews called the Mountain of the House of the Lord into a Mountain of Corruption, and the fruitful tree of Worship into a barren tree of Superstition. In plain prose Jesus is said by the Synoptists to have denounced the Temple, saying that there should not be left of it "one stone upon another." He also spoke of it as "a den of robbers." He included it in His parable of the vineyard of which the labourers refused to give fruits to the vineyard's lord. It does not require a great stretch of imagination to suppose that Jesus also called it "the fig-tree" with "leaves without fruit," and denounced it as such when He looked on it from Mount Olivet. If that is the fact, we are justified in believing that under the perplexing Marcan story of the literal withering of a fig-tree, a parable is concealed[1]. The parable

---

[1] See *Son of Man* **3364** *i—q*. Also on "Monopolies" see *ib.* **3585** *c* shewing how "doves at one time were sold in Jerusalem for pence of gold" and how Rabban Simeon ben Gamaliel determined to break down this extortion so that "doves were sold that very day for two farthings." A passage in *J. Berach.* ii. 4 (teeming with quaint and ancient traditions

contained a condemnation by Jesus of all religious practices
that make an appointed place or time or bodily action—
appointed by "the commandments of men "—an essential of
worship. More especially is this condemnable when these
commandments are issued for their own interests by any class
of professional men (priests, prophets, magicians, ministers,
scribes, elders, or Pharisees) that professes to be intermediary
between God and the non-professional man.

How, if at all, does John intervene as to "this mountain "?
Not by any denunciations of the old Temple, which, when he
wrote, had long ago passed away. Not by any predictions of
its destruction except so far as they are conveyed in what
may be called the *fiat* implied in the words "Destroy this
temple." And, even there, destruction is overshadowed by
the thought of the reconstruction immediately predicted,
"In three days I will raise it up." No, in John's days, the
important thing was not to believe that the old Temple was
cast down but that the new Temple was built up, and was
to be kept pure and holy. "Make not my Father's house a
house of *merchandise*" was a precept needed for the Church
of Christ—no less than it had been for the Temple of

---

about the Messiah born in Bethlehem and snatched up "two days afterwards " to heaven) has (Ps. xxix. 5) " *The voice of the Lord breaketh the
cedars*. For one day He will destroy those who augment the prices in the
markets." Schwab's explanation of this mysterious passage is "They
stood in the markets, whose doors were made of cedar."

But is it not better to explain it from *J. Taanith* iv. 5 (6), as translated
in *Hor. Heb.* i. 87, " *Two cedars* were in the Mount of Olivet, under
one of which were four shops, where all things needful for purifications
were sold: out of the other, they fetched, every month, *forty seahs of
pigeons*, whence all the women to be purified were supplied "? These three
quotations are all from the Jerusalem Talmud, which would naturally be
more likely than the Babylonian Talmud to retain first-century traditions
of Jerusalemite practice in connection with the Temple. The same kind
of metaphor that explains the Jewish use of "this sycamine-tree " to
mean the abominable worship on Mount Gerizim, appears to be latent in
the grim application of " breaketh the cedars " to the destruction of the
abominable extortions on Mount Olivet.

Jehovah—in the days of false teachers and false apostles who had begun already to "*make-merchandise*" of the faithful[1].

In the Johannine dialogue on "this mountain" there is a condemnation of what may be called "the religion of the barren fig-tree"—words without works. What materials the Evangelist may have had for this dialogue between Jesus and the Daughter of Samaria—obviously symbolical in its mention of the five husbands[2] and in other details—we may not be able exactly to ascertain; but it appears to teach with a plain and simple directness the spiritual truth that was obscured and made almost entirely unintelligible for Greeks by the Marcan metaphor of the withering of the fig-tree erroneously interpreted as literal fact. It teaches us that we are to worship God with a worship that allows nothing in the province of the senses to come between us and Him saying to us "I am necessary to you as a mediator between you and God." Christians as well as Samaritans may make "this

---

[1] Jn ii. 16, 2 Pet. ii. 3 "and in covetousness shall they with feigned words *make-merchandise* of you." The spuriousness of the Epistle does not diminish its value as a testimony to what was going on at the beginning of the second century. Similar warnings, or implications, may be found in the Pauline Epistles. Comp. 2 Cor. xii. 18 "Did Titus take any advantage of you?"

[2] See *Enc. Bibl.* "Gospels" col. 1801—2 for parallelisms between the Johannine Dialogue and passages in Philo about Moses sitting at the well; and about woman as the type of "sense"; and the "seducer" who acts through "the five senses" and leads the soul from "the lawful husband"; and idolatry as being the sin of "having many husbands"; and "believing on the report of a woman" (Jn iv. 42 believed "no longer owing to the speaking of the woman").

All these symbolical details do not at all prevent us from believing that John is here describing, in his own way and words, a journey of Jesus in the course of which—as might be said in Jewish idiom—"the Daughter of Samaria stretched out her hands to receive the living water from the Lord, after having played the harlot with many husbands and gone to the waters of Sychar (drunkenness)" (comp. Jer. ii. 13—25). Such a journey corresponds to the Mark-Matthew journey into the parts of Tyre and Sidon (omitted by Luke) in the course of which Jesus cast out a devil from the daughter of the Syrophoenician woman.

mountain"—some Christian Gerizim—a necessity for approaching God. We are warned against it. We are to worship Him "neither in *this mountain* nor in Jerusalem" but "in spirit and truth[1]."

§ 5. *The advantage of an inclusive study of such allusions*

All this language about "fig-trees" (or "sycamines" or "plane-trees") and "mountains" is so unlike anything in our experience that we naturally find difficulty at first in believing that it could exist[2]. Much less can we believe that it could

---

[1] See *Johannine Vocabulary* **1647** foll., which suggests that the original text gave the language of the Samaritan woman thus (Jn iv. 20, 22) "Our fathers [*i.e.* the Samaritans] worshipped in this mountain, and ye [Jews] say (that) '*In Jerusalem is the place where it is right to worship; ye [Samaritans] worship that which ye know not, we [Jews] worship that which we know—because salvation is of the Jews*'."

On this Samaritan representation of the arrogant and offensive language of the Jewish controversialists there follow words of peace (Jn iv. 21) "Jesus saith unto her, 'Woman, believe me, the hour cometh when neither in this mountain nor in Jerusalem shall ye worship the Father'."

Against the ordinary order there are these considerations. (1) It is (I believe) unique that Jesus should call His countrymen "the Jews"; (2) though it may be rhetorically defended (as it is by Chrysostom) Nonnus paraphrases "the Jews" by an emphatic "we"; (3) it is doubtful whether John would assent to the statement "Salvation is of the Jews," or (4) would represent Jesus as saying that He "worshipped"; (5) the language, if assigned to Jesus, is out of tune with the context, but (6) if assigned to the woman, is suitable to her desire to draw off the conversation to a national and controversial topic about which she might speak as an injured person ; (7) the sentence beginning "Ye worship that which ye know not" might naturally be transferred from the woman to Jesus by editors or scribes who did not perceive that the words were spoken by the woman bitterly and ironically in the character of controversialist "Jews."

[2] See, however, *Son of Man* **3364** *d* for scriptural personifications of "mountain" in Jer. li. 25 "I am against thee, O *mountain of destruction* (or, *corruption*)," and Zech. iv. 7 "Who art thou, O *great mountain.*" Comp. 2 K. xxiii. 13 "*mountain of destruction* (or, *corruption*)," Targ. "*mountain of Olives.*"

The peculiarity underlying the Synoptic use of "mountain" appears

give rise to serious error in the first century. But as soon as its frequency among later Jews is proved, and as soon as we see also an apparent allusion to it in the Fourth Gospel, then we perceive that its unlikeness to anything in Gentile literature would make it all the more likely to cause errors in the earliest extant attempt at a written gospel in Greek—a gospel that in its very first sentence contains an error that any educated Jew would immediately expose[1].

And, in the case of the "fig-tree" or "mountain" in Mark and Matthew, if we say "We refuse to believe anything so unlikely as that these terms could have been metaphorically used," we have to face the reply "Is it not still more unlikely that Jesus actually withered a fig-tree and promised His disciples that, in a literal sense, they, too, should 'do this deed of the fig-tree'?" And again, "Is it not also more unlikely that this extraordinary miracle should be omitted in Luke's parallel narrative? Does it not also require some explanation, that no Evangelist but Matthew adds the promise '*Ye shall do the deed of the fig-tree*,' to the promise which he and Mark mention about '*this mountain*,' where the parallel Luke has nothing but '*this* [or, *the*] *sycamine-tree*'?"

In concluding these remarks on the very difficult narrative in Mark, we must not forget that the passage does not stand alone, but as one of seven passages containing Marcan difficulties, in all the rest of which—though selected without any thought of Johannine intervention—we have found a strong probability that John has intervened.

It is not contended that in this last instance John's mention of "this mountain" has been *proved to be alluding to Mark's particular mention of "this mountain*," where Matthew adds,

---

to be that it was used alternatively with various forms of "*terebinth*," "*sycamine*," "*fig-tree*" derived from post-scriptural tradition.

[1] Mk i. 2 "Isaiah" for "Malachi and Isaiah." Jerome (on Mt. iii. 3) explains it as (1) "an error of scribes," or (2) an error caused by "making one *corpus*" out of "diverse testimonies."

and Luke has, a mention of a "tree." But it is contended that even in this instance—where, at first sight, we might have supposed the hypothesis of allusion to be absurd—it has been *proved to be not absurd*, so far as concerns a general parallelism between "mountain" and "tree," in a metaphorical sense, meaning corrupt worship, and *bringing out a doctrine of Christ's that had been merged in miracle by Mark.* In the rest of the instances, allusion appears to be either proved or probable. And in all, even in this last one, the hypothesis of a possible allusion seems to have been a fruitful one, inasmuch as it has turned our thoughts in a natural way to the varying thoughts of Christians in the first century, lifting us above the level of mere words to an appreciation of the spiritual source whence the words proceeded.

For these reasons, the results of our experiment should confirm us in our purpose to make the study of Johannine allusions to Marcan peculiarities a prominent part of our study of the Fourfold Gospel. For we have been led on by it, in an unexpected way, to see that in several instances the things that Mark has set down so obscurely or harshly as to induce Luke (and sometimes Matthew also) to alter them, are just the things in which first-century Christians (including the later Synoptists) would be greatly but diversely interested and in need of such help as a fourth evangelist might bestow. This help, we find, our Fourth Evangelist has in some cases actually bestowed.

These results justify us in giving special attention to Mark (rather than Matthew and Luke) in his relations to John. We will impartially keep our eyes open to John's allusions to any one of the three Synoptists. But we shall not be unfair if we give special care and more space to his allusions to Mark.

The reason will be that they will demand more care and space. But the additional care and space will be devoted, not to cherishing, but to testing, our hypothesis. As to Matthew and Luke, if we find John alluding to the peculiarities of either of them (in the course of the Synoptic Tradition), we shall put down the fact with ready recognition, though with surprise. But as to Mark we shall do more. We shall not only put down, without surprise, each instance where we find John alluding to him; but we shall also put down, subject to certain definite exceptions, *every instance where John does not allude to a Marcan peculiarity omitted or altered by Luke (with, or without, Matthew).*

"In these cases," we shall say, "the theory of Johannine intervention fails." No one surely can think that a theory subjected to such tests is inadequately tested.

CHAPTER V

THE COURSE OF PROCEDURE

§ I. *The advantages of taking Mark as the starting-point*

HAVING to study the Fourfold Gospel with a constant reference to the likelihood of Johannine allusions to Mark, shall we take John as our starting-point, and work upwards to his sources in Mark? Or shall we take Mark as our starting-point, and work downwards to the three streams—Matthew, Luke and John, streams all amplified from other than Marcan sources, but all, in some degree, flowing from Mark?

The latter is the more natural course and seems hardly to need justification. But it has many small disadvantages, which must receive careful consideration; and in view of these, it may be well here to restate, in two or three sentences, what are the great and solid reasons for taking Mark as the starting-point.

First, it has been shewn above that Mark contains a tradition from which Matthew and Luke borrowed, and in behalf of which John—whether deliberately or not—sometimes intervened. Secondly, it is also an undisputed fact that although Matthew singly, and Luke singly, may deviate from Mark's chronology, they never do so jointly. Thirdly, there are the advantages of Mark's frequent (though not invariable) brevity, and of his bluntness and freedom from apologetic bias or softening paraphrase. Lastly, we avoid some dangers—which might result from a Johannine starting-point—of straying into conjectures as to the "other than Marcan sources" from which John may have borrowed. A word on this subject may be in season here, just to explain that, if we pass it by, it will not be because we ignore it.

That there actually were—already in Luke's days—other than Marcan sources (and "many" of them, too) is demonstrable not only from the external testimony of Luke's Preface ("many have taken in hand") but also from the internal evidence of Luke's Gospel in which we find traces of different styles and different shades of thought. This is also true, to some extent, of Matthew's Gospel.

In the Fourth Gospel the existence of various sources is not recognisable from internal evidence; for the whole of it is written in one style and on one and the same level of mystical and allusive thought. Nevertheless we may be antecedently certain that John was not uninfluenced by those "many" evangelists whom Luke's Preface mentions. Most of them, probably, John would desire not to borrow from, but to guard his readers against. But from some he may not have disdained to borrow a fact, and from some a thought.

The first Epistle to the Corinthians reminds us that others beside Paul could say "my Gospel[1]." There was Apollos; there was Cephas[2]. The Preaching of Peter, or Cephas, is traditionally said to have been taken down in notes by Mark. But it must have left other memorials, remaining in the minds of many till the end of the first century, beside those inadequate Marcan records, if records they are. As for the Gospel of Apollos, it is one of the many marvellous silences of the first century that so successful and ardent a preacher— who, starting in Ephesus from "the baptism of John," "mightily confuted the Jews" in Achaia, and whom Paul mentioned to the Corinthians as on a footing with himself and Peter—so utterly disappeared from all subsequent

---

[1] Rom. ii. 16, xvi. 25 (comp. 2 Tim. ii. 8 and 1 Cor. xv. 1—8).
[2] 1 Cor. i. 12, iii. 4, 22.

Christian history that not a word remains, from Papias or any other Christian writer, early or late, to tell us any solid truth about his subsequent labours or even about the time of his death[1].

Apollos was an Alexandrian, and might be expected to shew traces of Philo's influence. Also, we should expect him to have dwelt upon "the baptism of John [the Baptist]." In these two respects the Gospel of Apollos might have had characteristics also to be found in the Gospel of John. But to do more than touch on these interesting facts—or rather, on these interesting and provoking absences of fact—would lead us quite away from our subject. We are dealing with the presence of fact, solid, demonstrated fact:—namely, the priority of Mark; the indebtedness of Matthew and Luke to Mark; and those other undoubted characteristics of Mark above mentioned, which distinguish him from the later Synoptists. These things make it desirable that Mark should stand first on those occasions on which we can construct four parallel columns of evangelical narrative or discourse, for the purpose of comparing them together.

§ 2. *The disadvantage of taking Mark as the starting-point*

Unfortunately Rushbrooke's Synopticon shews us that the "occasions on which we can construct four parallel columns of evangelical narrative or discourse," are extremely rare. The "four-column passages" include little· more than some of the acts and words of John the Baptist, the feeding of the five thousand, and the riding into Jerusalem. There are also short parallels in Christ's prediction of Peter's denial and its fulfilment; the arrest, trial, execution and burial

---

[1] Origen (on Rom. xvi. 10) asks whether "Apelles" is Apollos. Deissmann (p. 149) quoting a will dated 238—7 B.C. Ἀπολλώνιον...ὃς καὶ Συριστὶ Ἰωνάθας, says that the former "is a sort of translation" of the latter.

of Jesus; and a vision of angels at the sepulchre. In the story of the anointing of Jesus by a woman, John steps into the Synoptic tradition, but Luke steps out of it, giving a different story[1]. In the story of the walking on the waters, John intervenes, but Luke is silent[2].

To the "four-column passages" we might append the Johannine purification of the temple, and perhaps even the Johannine healing of an "impotent" man, as corresponding, in some sense, to narratives in the Synoptists, though not referring to identical events.

We have seen above that John appeared to intervene in at least five or six out of a group of seven instances where Mark contained something that might raise objections or difficulties. But the Johannine interventions were all very brief. We must expect them always to be brief. Parallelisms with Synoptic narrative and phrase in an evangelist who deliberately avoids Synoptic language and seldom trenches on Synoptic history, could not possibly extend to any great length. That, of course, will be disadvantageous to our procedure. It was a disadvantage, above, to introduce a discussion of so important a subject as the Withering of the Fig-tree by calling attention to an apparently insignificant peculiarity of Mark (who says that the withering was noticed "in the morning" of the next day, as compared with Matthew, who says that the tree "was withered immediately"). The same disadvantage will have to be faced again and again.

For example, Mark's opening words are "the *beginning* of the gospel," but he does not tell us what "the gospel" means, nor does he explain clearly and unambiguously what "the *beginning*" is. John's opening words are "In the *beginning* was the Word," and, though he never uses the word "gospel" from first to last, he goes on to teach us a gospel, or good tidings, of light and life, as proceeding from the

---

[1] Jn xii. 1—8, Lk. vii. 36—50.　　[2] Jn vi. 15—21.

Word. A little later on, according to Mark, the Baptist uses concerning Jesus the words "*coming behind me.*" Luke omits "*behind me.*" John represents the Baptist as not only using but repeating "*behind me*" and playing on it antithetically. This has been pointed out in Chapter I, and the reader is here asked to prepare himself not to reject the suggestion that John alluded to Mark's "*beginning* of the gospel" till he has considered the much stronger evidence indicating that John does allude to Mark's "coming *behind me.*" At the outset of the study of the Fourfold Gospel we are to keep our minds open to a cumulative demonstration that in a great number of instances (of which "the *beginning*" may be the first) John is trying (so to speak) to rehabilitate Mark, by putting new life and spiritual meaning into some of his obscure or prosaic expressions.

Many of these alleged rehabilitations, if they were taken singly, would seem so far-fetched as not to deserve consideration. For example, Mark, using the present tense, tells us that, at the Baptism of Jesus, the heavens were seen "*in the act of being rent asunder*"; but Matthew and Luke, using the past tense and a different verb, say that the heavens "*were opened.*" John does not mention this at the time, as he does not describe the Baptism of Jesus. But, a little afterwards, he represents Jesus as saying to His newly-formed band of disciples "Ye shall see the heaven [*permanently*] *opened* and the angels of God ascending and descending upon the Son of Man." In this, as in other cases, we must consider not only the words but the thought beneath the words; and if the hypothesis of allusion to Mark brings out an appropriate meaning in John, not seen before—a meaning appropriate to his context and to his Gospel as a whole, and appropriate to an evangelist supplementing earlier evangelists—we may reasonably add it to the instances of probable Johannine intervention.

If the criticism suggests itself, "Are you not evolving

something very subtle (your Johannine 'permanently open') out of something that is comparatively commonplace hyperbole (the Marcan 'being rent asunder')?" it will be a fair rejoinder to say, "Mark *is* often comparatively 'commonplace' and John *is* often comparatively 'subtle'; so that, if John interpreted Mark, this is just what might have been expected."

§ 3. *The disadvantage of neglecting Johannine chronology*

Another disadvantage of starting from Mark (or from any of the Synoptists) is that we may lose hold of the Johannine thought by giving up the Johannine, for the Synoptic, chronology. For example, John tells us that at the very beginning of His public work—not later on, after many conflicts with the rulers of the Jews, but in His very first collision with them—Jesus said to the Jews in the Temple, "Destroy this temple and in *three days* I will raise it up." At the same time John plainly warns us that the words were not literal but metaphorical and referred to His resurrection.

Now Mark, followed by Matthew, places similar words in the mouth of "false witnesses" at Christ's trial. Luke omits them altogether. This, then, is one of the clearest cases that can be alleged for the theory of Johannine intervention. But in what order are we to place it? If we delay to mention it till we come to it in Mark, we pass over one of the most important characteristics of the Johannine Gospel, namely, its recognition that Jesus, from the beginning, preached in some form the doctrine of "resurrection in *three days*" or "on *the third day*." This the Synoptists take literally, prefixing to the phrase "raised up in *three days*" predictions about being "killed" (or even "crucified"). These predictions they place at a comparatively late period in Christ's career.

It would seem that the Johannine tradition about "*three days*" ought to come before us at least twice. It must come

along with the Synoptic tradition about being killed and
"raised up in *three days*" or "on *the third day*." There we
shall compare both traditions with Hosea's prophecy, describing Israel as "smitten," but destined to be "raised up
on *the third day*" and to "live" in the sight of the Lord[1].
But it ought also to come before us along with the Synoptic
accounts of Christ's trial and crucifixion. For there, in Mark
and Matthew, the charge of planning to destroy the Temple
and to raise up another, is twice mentioned—once in the trial
before the chief priests, and once as uttered by the servants of
the chief priests, when Jesus is hanging on the Cross. On
both occasions, the charge contains the clause "*in three days*."

Luke, on both occasions, omits it. Possibly he regards
the omission as justified because the chief priests themselves
regarded the words as so obviously metaphorical that they
based no charge upon them when they brought Jesus before
Pilate. Possibly, remembering how the Christians had
suffered under Nero, on the false charge of incendiarism,
Luke saw a disadvantage in repeating such baseless charges
against Christ—baseless, indeed, but nevertheless likely to be
caught up and repeated by the multitudes in the cities of the
Gentiles. For they could easily understand the accusation.
But they could not easily understand how the Christians explained it (or, as their enemies would say, explained it away).

John takes an opposite course. Instead of suppressing
a fabrication, or perversion, or misinterpretation—preserved
by Mark and Matthew but omitted by Luke—of words

---

[1] Hos. vi. 2 on which see *Paradosis* 1218, 1297, and especially 1306:
"As regards the meaning of the 'two days' and 'third day' in Hosea,
Jewish criticism is divided. Rashi refers it to the destructions of the
two temples and the future rebuilding of a third; others to the two
captivities; others to the interval between death and decomposition.
But Ibn Ezra, one of the most trustworthy critics on verbal points, says,
'*He will make us to live* means *He will heal us : In two days* means *In
a short time.*' This suggests a parallelism with a saying of our Lord
recorded by John alone, (xvi. 16) '*A little while* and ye shall see me'."

alleged to have been uttered by Jesus, without any mention of words like them *actually uttered* by Jesus, he gives us *actual words*, and dramatically represents them as being misinterpreted at the very moment of their utterance. To these he gives a prominent place at the very outset of his Gospel, as if saying to us "Observe from the beginning how the Lord set His thoughts on things above, on the spiritual Jerusalem, not on things below, not on the earthly Jerusalem, and how He merged Himself in the Church or Congregation or Temple of His Father, and how, in consequence, His gospel was misunderstood."

This mention of Christ's "gospel" suggests the propriety of yet another reference to the Johannine doctrine of the "*three days.*" Ought we not to mention it at the outset along with our sketch of what the four Evangelists meant by the "gospel"? Mark mentions "gospel" in his first verse, and often again, but never directly defines it. John never mentions it but is always leading us to think of it. In Mark, the context implies that the "gospel" is the good tidings prophesied by Isaiah, the return of the captives to Zion, ransomed, and healed from all their diseases—fulfilled more especially at first in the casting out of devils, but afterwards, rather unexpectedly, in the forgiveness of sins. In John, it is the restoration of Man to that likeness from which he fell after being created by the Father through the Son, so that men receive "authority to become children of God[1]." But in John it is also the fulfilment of the Promise to Abraham ratified by sacrifice, the Father sacrificing the Son, the Lamb of God. The water and the wine of Cana, at the beginning, predict, as it were, the shedding of the blood of that Lamb ; and the water and the blood from the Crucified, at the end, fulfil the prediction.

The same plan of iteration must be adopted as to other important subjects, and, in particular, the Eucharist. This

---

[1] Jn i. 12.

will not come before us, directly, in Mark's order, till the night of the Last Supper. But it will come before us indirectly through the eucharistic sign of the Feeding of the Five Thousand, in the following way. John agrees with Mark and Matthew in describing, immediately after that miracle, a storm (omitted by Luke) from which the disciples —on their way to Gennesaret or Capernaum in a boat—are delivered by Jesus who appears to them walking on the sea. At the end of this narrative Mark and Matthew and John say severally :—

Mk vi. 51–2	Mt. xiv. 32–3	Jn vi. 21
And he went up to them into the boat. And the wind abated. And they were exceedingly amazed in themselves. *For they understood not concerning the loaves,* but *their heart was* (or, *had been*) *hardened.*	And when they went up into the boat the wind abated. But those in the boat worshipped him, saying, Truly, thou art God's Son.	They were desirous therefore to take him into the boat. And immediately the boat was by the land to which they were going.

This remarkable Marcan insertion about "*the hardening of the heart*," in connection with the Feeding of the Five Thousand, must be compared with another, referring to, and placed almost immediately after, the Feeding of the Four Thousand, an event not narrated by Luke and John. As before, the "hardening," which Matthew again omits, is connected with "loaves" :—

Mk viii. 17–18	Mt. xvi. 8–9
Why reason ye because ye have no loaves? Do ye not yet perceive neither understand? *Have ye your heart hardened?* Having eyes see ye not, and having ears hear ye not? And do ye not remember...?	Why reason ye among yourselves, O ye of little faith, because ye have no loaves? Do ye not yet perceive neither remember...?

45

In the first of these two Marcan passages, the usual explanation of "understood not concerning the loaves" is given by Prof. Swete thus:—"Their amazement would have been less had they realised the wonder of the preceding miracle: 'debuerant a pane ad mare concludere' (Bengel). Somehow the miracles connected with the multiplication of food failed to impress the Twelve (cf. viii. 17 ff.); perhaps their administration of the food diverted their thoughts from the work wrought by the Lord."

But it is difficult to imagine how men of ordinary intelligence, knowing that they had but a supply of "five loaves" in one case and "seven" in another, could allow their "administration of the food"—to "five thousand" and "four thousand" men respectively ("besides women and children")—to "divert their thoughts from the work wrought by the Lord."

It is perhaps conceivable that, among the five thousand and more who partook of the loaves, some never knew and never asked whence the loaves came; but even as to these, the five thousand recipients, John says that "the men, seeing the signs that he had wrought, began to say, This is truly the Prophet that is to come into the world." And if even these men were so impressed by it, how could it "fail to impress" the disciples, who (according to John) must have heard Andrew and Philip bluntly expressing their sense of the impossibility of feeding such a multitude in the wilderness, and who (according to the Synoptists) had themselves expressed the same opinion?

Moreover, against this popular view there are the following objections, some of a critical nature, but some moral. First, the context of the second Marcan instance—though certainly confused and apparently halting between two interpretations—appears to blame the disciples, not for failing to understand that Jesus could at any time make five loaves feed five thousand people, or, in other words, that He could do what He liked—but *for failing to understand that, when He said " beware of leaven,"*

*He was not thinking of material, but of immaterial, "leaven,"
namely, hypocrisy.*

It does not obviously seem a sign of a "hardened heart"
if the disciples of the Lord Jesus failed—as Bengel puts it—
to "infer from the bread to the sea." For did not their Master
Himself say, later on, "*If* it be *possible*," and does not Mark
say that, on a certain occasion, He "*was not able* to do any
mighty work"? But it might seem to a spiritual Messiah
a sign of "a hardened heart," if His disciples interpreted His
Eucharistic doctrine of self-sacrifice, taught in the Feeding
of the Five Thousand, as meaning "a doctrine of loaves and
fishes." After all that Jesus had done and taught, might it not
seem to Him a hard thing that even the Twelve should so mis-
understand Him as to suppose that His mission was merely
to bring peace and plenty and political freedom to His
countrymen—giving up the hopes of that new Commonwealth
in which the citizens were to see the "heaven" always "open,"
and "the angels of God ascending and descending on the
Son of Man"?

Now this misunderstanding, according to John, did actually
possess the great mass of the Jews who partook of the
mystery of the Feeding of the Five Thousand. They entirely
missed its meaning. John alone describes the failure that
followed, and the attempt to make Christ a king, and His
consequent withdrawal from the multitude. We shall have
to consider whether John is not right, and all the Synoptists
wrong—Mark being the only one of them who retains a
vestige of the truth. If we decide in favour of John, we shall
have to go further and reject the Marcan and Synoptic view
—or at all events the view that would naturally be attributed
to the Synoptists, if John had not written—that Jesus never
spoke of the mystical bread of the brethren till the night on
which He was delivered up.

Not indeed that we must consequently accept, as coming
from the lips of the historical Jesus, every word of that long

discourse about the mystical Bread which John puts into His mouth as being uttered in the synagogue at Capernaum, almost immediately after the Sign of the Five Thousand. But though we reject the words, we shall be prepared to accept the thought. Piecing together Marcan scraps of tradition with the aid of what we may call John's Targumistic exposition of it, we shall (I believe) arrive at the conclusion that a Eucharistic doctrine expressed in a Eucharistic practice was inculcated by Jesus at an early period[1], and only repeated with special emphasis—not introduced as a quite novel thing —on the night of the Last Supper[2].

---

[1] Nothing in this section is intended to suggest that John regarded the Feeding of the Five Thousand as being a mere metaphor treated as literal fact. The *consensus* of the Four Gospels does not permit us to place this narrative on the same level as that of the Withering of the Fig-tree, omitted by Luke and John. John (doubtless) accepted the Feeding as what is called a miracle. He differs from the Synoptists merely in insisting that it is a *moral* or *spiritual* miracle, a "sign."

This is not the place to discuss what, if any, material action—that is to say, what, if any, actual feeding of a multitude—may have accompanied what Mark (vi. 34) and Luke (ix. 11) severally call Christ's "teaching many things" and "speaking concerning the kingdom of God." This must be discussed hereafter when we come to the subject in its Synoptic order.

[2] Comp. *Acts of John* § 8, which says that, when Jesus was invited by a Pharisee to a meal, the disciples went with Him; then Jesus "used to receive one loaf" (as also did the other guests) "and blessing His own loaf He used to distribute it to us, and from this slight [nourishment] each was filled." This quaint materialisation may indicate an early and habitual use of the sign of "*one loaf.*" This will come before us in considering Mk viii. 14 "and they forgot to take loaves *and had but one loaf with them in the boat.*" Matthew omits the italicised words and Luke omits the whole, so that, according to our rule, John should intervene. John nowhere mentions "*one* loaf." But he describes "a fish" and "*a loaf*" as prepared for the disciples in the course of Christ's final manifestation, during which "Jesus cometh, and taketh *the loaf,* and giveth to them, and the fish likewise." See Jn xxi. 9 foll., where R.V. text has "*bread*," but R.V. marg. "*a loaf.*" The latter rendering is favoured by the parallelism between it and "*a fish.*" See *Son of Man* **3422** *i.*

48

These instances must suffice to shew both the disadvantage —and also the means by which we may hope to minimise the disadvantage—of subordinating the chronology of John to that of Mark.

§ 4. *The disadvantage of passing over traditions outside the threefold Synoptic Tradition*

Near the opening of Mark, where he represents the Baptist as saying about the Messiah " He shall baptize you with the Holy Spirit," Matthew continues, and Luke, too, almost identically, with an insertion of some length :—" *and with fire, whose winnowing-fan is in his hand...unquenchable fire.*" Mark omits this double tradition of Matthew and Luke. John, too, omits it. And the question arises whether we are, or are not, to include in our investigation passages of this kind, where John agrees with Mark in omitting what is in Matthew and Luke. May we say that we have here four evangelists two of whom agree in inserting, and two in omitting, an important clause in John the Baptist's description of his successor's baptism ? And should this clause be treated as a part, though a disputed part, of the Fourfold Gospel ?

On the whole, we shall decide in the affirmative here, for including the passage[1]. But it will only be on the ground that it is so closely connected with the Marcan tradition that it may be regarded as completing a sentence in Mark. If it had not this close connection, we should have to treat it like the Lord's Prayer, and the Beatitudes, and other passages collected by Matthew in the Sermon on the Mount and dispersed by Luke throughout his Gospel in various settings —that is to say, as part of that Double Tradition of Matthew and Luke which lies altogether outside Mark, and which is

---

[1] If we did not include it here, we might include it in later comment on Mk ix. 49 "salted with fire," omitted by the parall. Matthew, and also by Luke.

commonly called "Q," and recognised by many as a separate book[1]. This mass of tradition lies beyond our present scope and requires examination in a separate treatise. In such a separation we may acquiesce all the more readily because John very rarely borrows from, or alludes to, the Double Tradition of Matthew and Luke[2].

It will often be found, however, that the germ of some finely and fully expressed doctrine in the Double Tradition of Matthew and Luke lies buried in one of the short and obscure sayings in Mark. Wherever this is the case, we shall prefer to err on the side of insertion rather than that of omission. To take an extreme case, when we come to the Mark-Matthew narrative about the healing of the daughter of a Syrophoenician woman at a distance, through the mother's faith—in the course of a northern journey of Jesus wholly omitted by Luke—we shall compare it, not only with the Johannine narrative of a "nobleman's" son healed at a distance through the father's faith, but also with the narrative, in the Double Tradition, of the healing, at a distance, of a centurion's servant (*or*, boy) through the centurion's faith. We shall also compare and contrast the Synoptic cure of the paralysed man, whose sins are remitted, with the Johannine cure of the "impotent" man who, after being cured, receives the warning "Continue no longer in sin."

Again, in discussing the Marcan account of the calling of the earliest Apostles, while pointing out the very different aspect of the Johannine account, we shall also call attention to the Lucan narrative of a miraculous draught of fishes,

---

[1] On "Q," or the Double Tradition of Matthew and Luke, see *Son of Man* **3333** *a—d*.

[2] See *Son of Man* **3432** *b* on Lk. xiv. 26, "one of the very few passages where John takes up a phrase peculiar to Luke," namely, "hateth...his own soul." It is rightly printed in Rushbrooke's *Synopticon* as part of the Double Tradition, though the harshness of "hate" has been softened in the parallel Mt. x. 37.

which Luke alone connects with the calling of Peter, and shall note its similarity to a Johannine narrative of a miraculous draught of fishes, in which Peter plays a prominent part, after the Resurrection. And when we discuss the brief Marcan statement about the naming of Peter ("and Simon he surnamed Peter") we shall refer not only to John's tradition "thou shalt be called Cephas" but also to Matthew's much fuller tradition about "Peter" and the "building" of the "Church."

§ 5. *The advantages outweigh the disadvantages*

Thus we shall try to minimise in practice the disadvantages of taking Mark as our starting-point. The disadvantages are numerous and obvious. But on the other side we shall have (as was stated at the beginning of this Chapter) the great gain of a simple, compendious, definite, and impartial standard by which to test the theory of Johannine intervention in behalf of Mark. The adoption of the Marcan order, Mark being accompanied by the parallel Luke, will bring before us regularly and inevitably every instance where Luke omits or alters a Marcan tradition. In each case we shall be bound to find, either some Johannine intervention, or some reason for non-intervention. By degrees the reasons for non-intervention will in some cases make themselves clear. For example, we shall find that John never mentions exorcism, or leprosy, or Herodianism, or any of the Herods, or passages favouring the identification of the Baptist with Elijah.

About Marcan passages bearing on these subjects the reader will be prepared to find that, even though Luke differs from Mark, John is silent. Other instances of Johannine silence will occur, some of them only poorly explicable, others not at all. These will be called failures. Against the failures the reader will be able to reckon up the successes and to strike a balance. The constant presence of a simple standard, ensured by starting from so unsophisticated a writer as Mark, appears to be an advantage—for our purpose of dispassionate investigation into the relation between the Three Synoptists and so subtle and perplexing a writer as the Fourth Evangelist—quite great enough to outweigh all the above-mentioned disadvantages.

CHAPTER VI

"PARALEIPOMENA" OR "THINGS OMITTED"

I. *John regarded as a book, like Chronicles, "supplying things omitted*[1]*"*

WE have seen that internal evidence supports external evidence in the conclusion that John supplements the Synoptists; and any one can verify for himself the conclusion that Chronicles supplements Kings. John, therefore, in supplementing, had before him a precedent of scriptural authority. Are there reasons for thinking that he was influenced by it? If so, in what direction would the influence tend? Or how does it appear to have actually tended?

The answer is, that John and the Chronicler, though alike in much that they do, are utterly unlike in their way of doing it. Both of them supplement; both of them omit; both of them comment, and occasionally (we may venture to say) both of them correct. But their supplements, their omissions, their comments, and their corrections, are of a different kind. Nevertheless their likeness, in respect of occasional correction, ought to teach us so much as this, that if the Old Testament writer allowed himself to alter the language of the ancient scriptures known as the Books of the Kings[2], in order to make it here and there more edifying (as it seemed to him), New Testament evangelists might be expected to do this

---

[1] On "Paraleipomena," *Things Omitted*, as the title of Chronicles in LXX, see above, p. 15.

[2] See p. 15, n. 1.

with much more freedom, as long as "the gospel" was fluid (being largely oral) and before a few written gospels had achieved a pre-eminent position that had begun to give them the same kind of authority among Christians that the Old Testament possessed among Jews in the first century.

In the Old Testament, the Chronicler largely retains the language of Kings, but freely corrects phrases, and sometimes statistics, apparently with a view to exaltation of his subject. Similarly, in the New Testament, Matthew and Luke often freely patch, so to speak—correcting a phrase or two of their predecessor Mark, but retaining his verbal context. John does not patch in this way. On the occasions when he appears to be intervening, he for the most part avoids the language of all his predecessors. Often he seems to be explaining Mark rather than correcting either Mark, or Matthew, or Luke.

This is what might be expected, if we take into consideration the difference between the Chronicler's and the Evangelist's environments (not to speak of the difference between their characters). The Chronicler probably had little reason to fear serious criticism if he exalted the majesty of God by a few alterations of the text of Kings. But John appears to have written at a time when sharp criticism might be apprehended from those inside, as well as from those outside, the Church, if he favoured one Evangelist so far as to put others in the wrong. Outside, there loomed on the horizon the prospect of attacks (such as were made later on by Celsus and, later still, by Porphyry) on evangelic inconsistencies. Inside, there were those who said, in a contentious way, "I am of Paul," and "I of Apollos," and "I of Cephas." Each preached "the Christ," but on lines of his own. And superficial Christians, of a sectarian turn, who did not go down to "the Christ" that was at the root of these apostolic or quasi-apostolic "gospels," would be always on the alert to fasten on some external Pauline, Apollonian, or Petrine difference of phrase, or of arrangement, or of emphasis, which seemed to them to distinguish from all others the evangelist whom they preferred, and to make him the unique depository of the truth. Hence would arise a greater need for caution— so far as concerned the avoidance of discrepancies from early traditions—in the Fourth Evangelist than in the Three; and hence even in one of the points in which the Chronicler and John resembled each other—both being correctors of old traditions—there might naturally be a great difference in the execution of the task.

§ 2. *The historian's right to omit*

The very first words of Chronicles are worth a volume of evidence as to Jewish canons of the right of a historian to omit. "Adam, Seth, Enosh"—why is Cain omitted? No doubt because none of his posterity survived the deluge, so that his descendants could play no part, either as friends or as enemies, in the history of Israel. Again, Elijah occurs in Chronicles only as the author of "a writing" that came to Jehoram, the son of Jehoshaphat, prophesying his chastisement[1]. One might have supposed that if this was worth chronicling, space might have been found for the mention of Elijah's ascent to heaven, or for the vision that brought the "still small voice." But the author probably felt that the Law, and not the Prophets, must occupy his attention. It was his object to point a national moral: "When Israel obeyed the Law, there was prosperity; when Israel disobeyed, there was punishment." He has little to do with personal morality. The name of Uriah occurs in Chronicles only as one of David's "mighty men." Absalom—mentioned in Samuel and Kings more than a hundred times—occurs in the Chronicler's history of David only once[2]. But thus,

---

[1] 2 Chr. xxi. 12.

[2] 1 Chr. xi. 41 "Uriah the Hittite," 1 Chr. iii. 2 "the third, Absalom the son of Maacah."

in ignoring everything that is personal, and not directly conducive to the exaltation of the Law, the author, himself by nature prosaic, omits almost everything that is poetic, dramatic, and picturesquely typical. About the building of the material Temple he is as full and detailed as is the author of Kings, but about many of the most beautiful and personal histories that went far toward building up the national literature, and, through the literature, the nation itself, the Chronicler is silent.

John, too, omits much that is personal in the Synoptists, including the calling of what may be called the minor Apostles, with their several names[1]. He omits also all accounts of exorcism, including the story of the "Legion," and that of the father who cried, "I believe, help thou mine unbelief." No "publican," no "sinner," is mentioned as experiencing Christ's forgiving influence[2]. The identification of the Baptist with Elijah is denied at the beginning of the Gospel and never referred to afterwards. All the Herods are absent. And about the picturesque story of the sacrifice of the Baptist to the dancing of the daughter of Herodias John is no less silent—and perhaps no less contemptuously sceptical of the genuineness of the tetrarch's prearranged "oath"—than is (apparently) Josephus[3].

The result, however, of many of these omissions of Marcan personal detail—and in particular those that concern Herod Antipas—is not to make the Fourth Gospel impersonal, but to concentrate the interest on one Person. The Chronicler omits everything that does not point toward the Law; the Evangelist, everything that does not point toward the Son, who is the Light, and the Life, of the world. The Chronicler

---

[1] But he refers to it (Jn vi. 70, " Have not I chosen you, the Twelve ? ").

[2] John does not mention "publicans" at all. And "sinner" is only mentioned (Jn ix. 16, 24, 25, 31) in the charge of being "a sinner," brought against Christ Himself!

[3] Mk vi. 17—26, Mt. xiv. 3—9, see *Son of Man* **3338** *b*.

omits "Cain," because Cain does not point toward the Law. But the Evangelist, being a poet (that is, a "maker[1]"), and in harmony with the Maker of the world, knows that the light shines in darkness, and that darkness must not be omitted in the opening words of his Gospel, describing the second genesis of Man, or the building of the New Temple. The "darkness" increases the glory of the victorious light : "The light shineth in the darkness and the darkness overcame it not." The Evangelist does not omit the name of Judas but emphasizes it. And although he does not repeat the lengthy Marcan details about John the Baptist's imprisonment and death, he does not leave his readers in ignorance of the fact that he is passing over them (" John was not yet cast into prison ").

As regards the personal element, nowhere in the Synoptists are new characters introduced so freely—in places, sometimes, where the Synoptists have mutes or unnamed speakers or a blank :—Mary Magdalene, Mary the sister of Martha, Andrew, Philip, Nathanael, Nicodemus, Jude, and Thomas, not to speak of the unnamed woman of Samaria ; and yet all these new characters, instead of distracting, attract and concentrate our attention on the central character, the Son, the Life, and the Light.

---

[1] Compare Wordsworth's *Prelude* v. 595 foll. on :

> "the great Nature that exists in works
> Of mighty Poets. Visionary power
> Attends the motions of the viewless winds,
> Embodied in the mystery of words."

If we bear in mind that *one and the same word* in Hebrew means "spirit," and "breath," and (often) "wind," we shall perceive in this passage a sympathy (perhaps unconscious) with the Johannine doctrine about (Jn iii. 8) the "wind," or "spirit," which, though "viewless," is heard as it "bloweth" (or "breatheth") where it "listeth." "The mystery of words" suggests the mystery of "the Word," and the mystery of the connection between the Word and the Spirit. And "visionary power" is a title that might be given to the whole of the Fourth Gospel.

§ 3. *Miracles omitted*

Both the Chronicler and John omit almost all the miracles
described by their predecessors. But the reason seems to be,
not that the miracles appeared to them incredible or doubtful,
but that they occupied a position too spacious and prominent
in the ancient books to allow of their insertion in a supple-
mentary book. Often, too, the contexts of the miracles fell
outside the province of the later writer. For example, the
Chronicler occupies himself mostly with Judah, not with
Israel. Hence he omits the seven miracles of Elijah and the
fourteen miracles of Elisha wrought during the reigns of Ahab
and his successor. But when Jehoshaphat king of Judah
comes and allies himself with Ahab king of Israel, then the
Chronicler does not omit the prophecy uttered in the presence
of both kings by Micaiah the son of Imlah concerning
the defeat and death of Ahab. In the conclusion of the
story, however, where the older writer says that "the dogs
licked up his [*i.e.* Ahab's] blood...according to the word of
the Lord which he spake" (referring to a previously recorded
prophecy of Elijah " In the place where dogs licked the blood
of Naboth, shall dogs lick thy blood") the later writer omits
this, while he inserts the comparatively uninteresting fulfilment
of Micaiah's prophecy. So also does he omit the miraculous
element contained in the older history of Jeroboam, the first
king of schismatic Israel. He deals as little as possible with
schismatic Israel and as much as possible with Judah.

In one instance, where he omits a miracle in connection
with the healing of Hezekiah, he at all events states that a
miracle did take place[1]; but he subordinates God's prophet

---

[1]   2 Kings xx. 1—11.   2 Chr. xxxii. 24.

In those days was Hezekiah   In those days was Hezekiah
sick unto death...(8) And Hezekiah   sick even unto death ; and he prayed
said unto Isaiah, What shall be the   unto the Lord ; and he spake unto
sign that the Lord will heal me...   him and [he] *gave him a sign* (or,

to God Himself, and omits all the picturesque details of the healing and of the "sign," hastening on to explain that Hezekiah "rendered not again according to the benefit done unto him," and giving an erroneous impression that God revealed His will directly to Hezekiah by some voice or vision, and not through Isaiah.

John omits all the acts of exorcism, and all the miracles of healing, described by the Synoptists. But, with two exceptions, we may say that he does not omit any miracle, recorded by any predecessor, in such circumstances and with such similarity of context as to force us to the conclusion that he rejected it. The two exceptions are, 1st, Peter's walking on the waves, recorded by Matthew alone, 2nd, the healing of the ear of the High Priest's servant, recorded by Luke alone.

In the former, the following parallels will shew the similarity of context in Matthew and John, and the incompatibility of the Petrine episode with the Johannine account :—

Mt. xiv. 27—32	Jn vi. 20—21
But straightway Jesus spake unto them, saying, Be of good cheer, It is I, fear not...But Peter answering him...(31) O thou of little faith, why didst thou doubt? (32) *And when they* (i.e. *Jesus and Peter*) *went up into the boat*, the wind abated.	But he saith unto them, It is I, fear not. *They desired therefore to take him into the boat*, and immediately the boat was by (*lit.* on) the land to which they were going.

Now that it is difficult or impossible in any reasonable way to reconcile Matthew's "*when they went up into the boat*"

(11) And Isaiah the prophet cried unto the Lord; and he *brought the shadow ten steps backward, by which it had gone down on the dial of Ahaz.*

wonder). But Hezekiah rendered not...

Who—in Chronicles—"spake" unto whom? Most English readers would probably reply "*God* spake to *Hezekiah*." But Rashi takes it as meaning "*Hezekiah* spake unto *God* [saying, What shall be the sign?] And the Lord gave him a sign"—interpreting Chronicles by Kings.

with the Johannine "*they desired therefore to take him into the boat*" may be inferred from the fact that even the ingenuity of the Diatessaron finds itself unable to insert the latter, though it does insert the following words "*and immediately the boat... they were going.*" It has been mentioned elsewhere[1] that the phrase about "taking him into the boat" appears to be a form of a Marcan tradition placed by Mark in the Stilling of the Storm but by John in the Walking on the Waters. It should also be noted that John would have, in favour of the omission of the Petrine episode, the direct testimony of Mark, who not only omits it but also writes "*And he* (i.e. *Jesus*) went up to them into the boat, and the wind abated"—not, as Matthew, "*they* went up." It is reasonable to conclude that John rejected this miracle, not as being incredible in itself, but as being at all events out of place here and contradicted directly as well as indirectly by Mark.

In the second instance, the healing of the High Priest's servant[2], it is worth considering whether mystical reasons may not have united with textual ones to induce John to omit the miracle. The Synoptic contexts exhibit an unusual degree of similarity in describing how one of those near Jesus, in the moment of His arrest, struck off the ear of the servant of the High Priest. Luke calls it "the right ear[3]," and adds " But Jesus answering said, *Suffer ye thus far*, and having touched the ear he healed him."

In place of this miracle, Mark has a blank. But Matthew has "Then saith Jesus to him, *Put up thy sword into its place....*"

Turning now to John we find, first, that he agrees with Luke in the mention of the "*right* ear"—*an agreement with Lucan narrative* (as distinct from that of Mark and Matthew)

---

[1] See pp. 25—6.

[2] Lk. xxii. 50—51, comp. Mk xiv. 47, Mt. xxvi. 51—2, Jn xviii. 10—11.

[3] On "the right ear" mentioned in the consecration of priests, see Exod. xxix. 20 (twice), Lev. viii. 23, 24 &c.

rare or non-existent elsewhere in Johannine narrative[1]. Secondly, John agrees with Matthew as to the command to sheathe the sword, though expressed in slightly different language ("put the sword into the sheath"). He is also the first to tell us that the unnamed disciple was "Simon Peter," and that the High Priest's servant was named "Malchus." But, about a miracle of healing, not a word : "Simon Peter therefore having a sword, drew it, and struck the servant of the high priest and cut off his right ear (now the servant's name was Malchus); Jesus therefore said to Peter, *Put the sword into the sheath....*"

A detailed explanation of these parallelisms must be deferred till we come to the passage in its Marcan order, but an outline may be given here.

(1) The words were simply a command to the disciples to desist—either "*Thus far*" by itself, or "*Thus far*" preceded by "*Let be!*", meaning "*Let be! Thus far* [and no further]."

(2) This, in effect, meant "*Enough of this*[2]!" Of this, Luke gives another version a little before, "Here are two swords. But he said to them, *It is enough*[3]."

(3) Compare Kings and Chronicles, identical as to the words "*It is enough :* now stay thine hand," but divergent in the sequel thus :—

Kings	Chronicles
So the Lord was intreated for the land, and the plague was stayed from Israel.	And the Lord commanded the angel ; and *he put up his sword again into the sheath thereof*[4].

---

[1] Agreement as to the *words* of Jesus (*e.g.* Jn xii. 25, Lk. xiv. 26, see p. 50, n. 2) is to be distinguished from agreement in *narrative*.

[2] In Lk. xxii. 51, the Syro-Sinaitic version has (Burkitt) "*Enough. As far as this* [man]"; Walton has Syr. "satis est ad hanc usque rem [processisse], Arab. "cohibe te," Aethiop. "sine hunc," Pers. "usque ad hunc terminum"; codex *b* has "dimitte eum" before the miracle, and "sine usque hoc" after it.

[3] Lk. xxii. 38. The Hebrew in Kings and Chron. ("*enough*, stay now thy hand") is the same as that used by Delitzsch ("*enough* for you") to render "*As far as this*" in Lk. xxii. 51.

[4] 2 S. xxiv. 16, 25, 1 Chr. xxi. 15, 27.

(4) Matthew, followed by John, interpreted the obscure words as a command about the sword, like that in Chronicles, " Restore it [*i.e.* the sword] to its sheath." Then they added, severally, traditions about the reason for the command— Matthew, "they that take...by the sword "; John, "the cup... shall I not surely drink it?"

(5) But Matthew, instead of " sheath" or " scabbard," has "*place.*" This shews how an original command in the form " Be it restored to its *place* ! "—meaning " Back with *the sword* to its place ! "—might be misunderstood as meaning " Let *the ear* be restored to its place[1]."

(6) Luke takes it thus, and clears away (as he supposed) the obscurity, saying, in effect, " Jesus not only said *Let* [*me go*] *as far as this* [*man*], but also went up to the man and touched him. And the consequence of the touch was an act of healing[2]."

Why does John follow Luke in the little detail of "the *right* ear," while rejecting Luke's miracle? Probably because he is preparing his readers for the trial of Christ before that Caiaphas who said to the chief priests "It is expedient that one man should die for the people." " These Jewish High Priests," John seems to say, "were wicked in the worst sense, far worse than Pilate. They were given over by God to pronounce a verdict in accordance with their ingrained injustice—externally High Priests of the Lord but internally ministers of Satan, 'the ruler of this world.' Most appropriately therefore was their servant and representative called ' Malchus' or ' King[3].' And, when this servant of theirs went forth to lay hands on Jesus, most appropriately was his 'right'

---

[1] Compare Jer. xlvii. 6 with Ezek. xxi. 30 Heb. "Cause it to return into its sheath," LXX ἀπόστρεφε, see context.

[2] Ephrem (pp. 236—7) says that the ear, as well as the sword, was " restored," *i.e.* brought back into its place.

[3] See Gesen. 573 foll. for many instances of names derived from the root of the Heb. "king."

ear cut off by the sword so that he lost that symbol of 'righteous hearing' which was bestowed by the Law of anointing on Aaron and his successors."

If the explanation outlined above is reasonable, it enables us to understand that John may have omitted this miracle, not only as a historian but also as a spiritual evangelist. He might conceivably have disguised his omission of it, by entirely passing over the circumstances of Christ's arrest. But this could not have been done without sacrificing important events in the Johannine context. And if John felt obliged to mention the wounding, and to leave out the healing, he seems to have done the best thing possible by suggesting that the healing, in the circumstances of the case, would have been spiritually and symbolically inappropriate.

§ 4. *Miracles inserted*

In Chronicles there are perhaps only two insertions of miracles in a context closely similar to the parallel context in Kings. Both of these refer to prayer "answered by fire[1]."

---

[1]

2 S. xxiv. 25.

(i) And David built there an altar unto the Lord, and offered burnt offerings and peace offerings. So the Lord was intreated for the land, and the plague was stayed from Israel.

1 Chr. xxi. 26—7.

And David built there an altar unto the Lord, and offered burnt offerings and peace offerings, and called upon the Lord; and *he answered him from heaven by fire* upon the altar of burnt offering. And the Lord commanded the angel; and he put up his sword again into the sheath thereof.

1 K. viii. 54—5.

(ii) And it was so, that when Solomon had made an end of praying all this prayer and supplication unto the Lord, he arose from before the altar of the Lord from kneeling on his knees with his hands spread forth toward heaven. And he stood

2 Chr. vii. 1—3.

Now when Solomon had made an end of praying, *the fire came down from heaven and consumed the burnt offering and the sacrifices*; and the glory of the Lord filled the house. And the priests could not enter into the house of the Lord,

It is probable that the Chronicler deliberately, but not dishonestly (from his point of view) added this because the consumption of sacrifice by fire from heaven was a part of the theophany in the dedication of the Tabernacle, and he could not bring himself to believe that it was not also a part in the dedication of the Temple. In Leviticus, it is mentioned along with, and as being distinct from, the appearance of " the glory of the Lord," as follows : " *The glory of the Lord appeared unto all the people. And there came forth fire from before the Lord, and consumed upon the altar the burnt offering and the fat* : and when all the people saw it, they shouted, and fell on their faces[1]."

If the author of the book of Kings knew of this Levitical description of " the glory of the Lord " and of " fire from before the Lord " in the Tabernacle, could he have omitted the latter, in his description of the dedication of the Temple, without some sense of the natural inference, namely, that the sanctity of the Temple was inferior to that of the Tabernacle ? Such a thought of inferiority—present to the minds of some at the laying of the foundations of the second Temple, into which no "glory of the Lord" entered at its dedication,

and blessed all the congregation of Israel with a loud voice, saying Blessed be the Lord...	because the glory of the Lord filled the Lord's house. And all the children of Israel looked on, *when the fire came down*, and the glory of the Lord was upon the house ; and they bowed themselves with their faces to the ground upon the pavement, and worshipped, and gave thanks unto the Lord, [saying] For he is good; for his mercy [endureth] for ever.

Both writers (1 K. viii. 10—11, 2 Chr. v. 11—14) have previously described "the cloud," or " the glory of the Lord," as " filling the house." But the peculiarity in the second narrative (ii) in Chronicles is this, that besides the "glory" of a visible " cloud," it speaks of a fire of a material kind, capable of consuming sacrifices.

[1] Lev. ix. 23—4.

nor was there any " fire from heaven[1] "—was assuredly not
present to the mind of the Chronicler in comparing the
Temple with the Tabernacle. This may be seen all through
his work, but more especially in his version of the words of
Solomon immediately preceding the passage under consideration. The ancient prayer of Solomon concludes with
a mention of Moses and the deliverance from Egypt. For
Moses, the Chronicler's version substitutes David. It concludes
with a quotation of three verses from the Psalm that describes
how David sought to " find a place for the Lord," and its last
words are " Remember the mercies of David thy servant[2]."

Before we pass to miracles inserted in the Fourth Gospel
it is natural to ask, " What did the Jews say, the Talmudists

---

[1] Ezra iii. 12, vi. 16. But 2 Macc. i. 18—36 contains a long account
of a continuation of the fire from the first Temple, by the agency of
Nehemiah.

Other apocryphal narratives shew the importance attached to the
continuation of the sacred fire, as to which note the variation in :—

Ezra vi. 3.	1 Esdr. vi. 24.
In the first year of Cyrus the king, Cyrus the king made a decree: Concerning the house of God at Jerusalem, let the house be builded, the place where they offer sacrifices, and let the foundations thereof be strongly laid ; the height thereof threescore cubits and the breadth thereof threescore cubits...	In the first year of the reign of Cyrus, king Cyrus commanded that the house of the Lord at Jerusalem should be built again, where they do sacrifice *with continual fire* ; whose height shall be sixty cubits and the breadth sixty cubits...

[2] 1 K. viii. 52—3.

	2 Chr. vi. 41—2.
That thine eyes may be open unto the supplication of thy servant, and unto the supplication of thy people Israel, to hearken unto them whensoever they cry unto thee. For thou didst separate them from among all the peoples of the earth, to be thine inheritance, as thou spakest *by the hand of Moses thy servant, when thou broughtest our fathers out of Egypt*, O Lord God.	Now therefore arise, O Lord God, into thy resting place, thou, and the ark of thy strength : let thy priests, O Lord God, be clothed with salvation, and let thy saints rejoice in goodness. O Lord God, turn not away the face of thine anointed: *remember the mercies of David thy servant* (see Ps. cxxxii. 1 foll., 8—10).

and Midrashists, about the omission, in Kings, of the descent of fire mentioned in Chronicles ?" The answer is noteworthy. There are several references in the Midrash to the narrative in Chronicles ; but I have not been able to find a single one that calls attention to the omission in Kings. In the whole of the Jerusalem Talmud there is no reference to the verses describing the descent of fire in Chronicles except for the purpose of defining the length of time necessary to constitute a religious act of prostration ; and in the Babylonian Talmud the only reference in the volumes hitherto (Jan. 1913) published by Goldschmidt repeats the same tradition though under the names of different Rabbis.

As regards miracles, then, our conclusion must be that the Jewish mind, so far as it is represented by the Chronicler, makes a marked distinction in favour of one that follows precedent and tends to edification.

Passing to John, we may say that with one exception, and that a slight one, John never inserts a new miracle in a Johannine passage that is parallel to Synoptic passages[1]. John introduces new miracles. But the Johannine miracles— or, as John calls them, "signs"—stand in a Johannine frame. They will therefore not be discussed here.

The one exception occurs in the Walking on the Waters, thus :—

Mk vi. 50–51	Mt. xiv. 27–32	Jn vi. 20–21
It is I, fear not. And he went up to them into the boat. And the wind abated.	It is I, fear not. But Peter...why didst thou doubt ? And when they had gone up into the boat the wind abated.	It is I, fear not; They therefore desired to take him into the boat, *and straightway the boat was by the land to which they were going.*

[1] On Jn xviii. 6, which I have not included, because some would not call it a miracle, see *Son of Man* **3326** *a*, which interprets it as a mis-understanding of an original tradition referring to the disciples (not the soldiers) who "fell back" and abandoned their Master.

What John inserts ("straightway the boat was *by* the land") is either hyperbole or miracle, and, as he is not given to hyperbole, the hypothesis of miracle is more probable. So regarded, it may be explained as a Johannine interpretation of a phrase in an obscure narrative, the whole of which is (1) omitted by Luke, (2) amplified with a Petrine insertion by Matthew, and therefore, we may reasonably infer, (3) much discussed in the first century.

It has been shewn in Johannine Grammar that the phrase "*on the sea*" may mean "*by the sea*," and that it has that meaning later on, where it is said that "Jesus manifested himself again to the disciples *on* (i.e. *by*) *the sea*[1]." In the present passage John uses the same preposition about "the land," clearly meaning, that the vessel was "*by*" (not "*on*") the land. And instead of saying that Jesus (or Jesus and Peter) "came into" the boat, he says simply that the disciples "desired *to take Jesus into the boat.*"

We have seen above that a clause of this kind is placed by Mark in another narrative. Some uncertainty about the arrangement of traditions at this point may have seemed to justify conjectural or probable alterations favourable to symbolism. John still retains the words "they behold Jesus... *becoming near the boat,*" but he uses them perhaps as we use language about "the land receding from our view" or "the land coming in sight." On this hypothesis, the meaning of the Johannine alterations may be something of this kind, "The disciples thought that the Lord was drawing near to them, but in fact He was drawing them to Himself. It was not needful that He should come up to them into the boat. It was not even needful that they should (as the Psalmist says) 'cry unto Him in their distress.' All that was needed was that they should 'desire' Him, as 'the haven where they

---

[1] *Johannine Grammar* **2340—6**. To the instances there given add Numb. xx. 24 (LXX) "*on* (i.e. *by* or *at*) the water," where another transl. has "*in.*"

desired to be.' That done, all was done, and the boat was safe by the shore[1]."

If this explanation is right, John shapes his account out of doubtful and variably reported traditions—not with a view to inserting, or to rejecting, the miraculous, but with a desire to tell a true story so as to bring out the depth and beauty of its truth.

§ 5. *The Passover*

Chronicles is one of the most prosaic works in the Old Testament, the Johannine Gospel is one of the most poetic works in the New. Yet the essential poetry in the shaping of Israel's history has constrained the Chronicler to give the same prominence as is given by the Evangelist to the same two great national symbols of the redeeming presence of the Lord and Saviour of the nation. These are the Passover and the Temple.

Of the first of these symbols, the Passover, the only express mention in Kings is in a brief edict of King Josiah, "Keep the passover unto the Lord your God, as it is written in this book of the covenant[2]," followed by a statement that "such a passover" had never before been celebrated, under "the judges," or "the kings of Israel," or "the kings of Judah[3]." Chronicles amplifies this with a detailed description of the actual celebration, but it omits the mention of "the kings of Judah[4]." Why is this? It is because Chronicles has already inserted a still fuller account of a celebration in the reign of Hezekiah, in which the voice of the Levites blessing

---

[1] Comp. Ps. cvii. 30 "So he bringeth them unto the haven where they desired to be," on which Jerome says that He who stills the storm, and to whom they desire to be led, is "the true haven."

[2] 2 K. xxiii. 21.   [3] 2 K. xxiii. 22.

[4] 2 Chr. xxxv. 18. It mentions "the days of Samuel" and "the kings of Israel," but not "the kings of Judah."

God's people "came up to his holy habitation, even unto heaven[1]."

Turning to the Gospels, we find that the Three, with the exception of a Lucan account of Jesus as a child of twelve going up to the Feast in Jerusalem, do not mention the Passover till their narratives bring them near the evening before the Crucifixion. But the Fourth Gospel places a Passover at an early period, and repeats a mention of it. It also prepares us, so to speak, for Paschal thoughts, even before Jesus has uttered a word, by introducing Him to us in the words "Behold the Lamb of God, which taketh away the sin of the world."

§ 6. *The Temple*

Next, as to the Temple. It is true that the details in Chronicles about the construction, ritual, and sacrifices of the Temple are prosaic and alien from Johannine thought. But toward the close of the book, the Chronicler is led by a sense of pathos into something like poetry. The Jews themselves, he says, "polluted the house of the Lord, which he had hallowed in Jerusalem"; they scoffed at the prophets, though the Lord had sent them "because he had *compassion* on his people *and on his dwelling place[2].*" The Lord's "compassion" for His "dwelling place" suggests a quasi-personification of the Temple which is brought out more clearly in the Fourth Gospel. Luke nowhere suggests such a thing. Mark and Matthew do indeed suggest the thought of a temple not made with hands, but only vaguely and in connection with what are called "false witnesses[3]". John expressly declares that Jesus, as one of His first acts, condemned the Jews for

---

[1] 2 Chr. xxx. 1—27. The whole of 2 Chr. xxix. 3—xxxi. 21 is devoted to Hezekiah's religious reformation, and there is no parallel to it in Kings (exc. a brief statement, about "high places &c.", in 2 K. xviii. 4).

[2] 2 Chr. xxxvi. 14—15.

[3] Mk xiv. 58, Mt. xxvi. 61, Lk. xxii. 66 foll. om.

making His Father's House "a house of merchandise," and predicted a New Temple, which He identified with "the temple of his body [1]."

Chronicles begins with "Adam" and ends with a royal proclamation about "building a house" for God: "All the kingdoms of the earth hath the Lord, the God of heaven, given me, and he hath charged me to build him an house in Jerusalem...Whosoever there is among you of all his people, the Lord his God be with him, and let him go up [2]."

Interpreted by a spiritual poet—not necessarily a Christian poet but a poet of the spiritual Israel—the opening as well as the closing words might point to the building up of Man as God's Temple. The first Adam was like Solomon's Temple, destined to fall, smitten by God's retributive wrath, but to be raised up again in a new Jerusalem, of which the name was to be "the Lord is there [3]."

Who was to rebuild the Temple in this new form? According to Chronicles, it was to be Cyrus. But spiritual Jews would recognise that in the first place, Cyrus was but an instrument in the hands of God, and, in the second place, such a temple as the Lord desired could be built by no mortal king, or king of the kingdoms of the earth. It was to be identified in some sense with Israel's Messiah or Anointed King. It was also to be "the meeting-place" of Jehovah and His purified Israel, the Bridegroom and the Bride, God and Man. Interpreted by spiritual Jews who were also Christians, this "temple" was no other than Jesus of Nazareth, who was at once the typical Son of Adam and the incarnate Son of God.

This essentially Hebrew and Jewish thought of the Temple as the centre of the national life, is wanting in Mark, except so far as it may be implied in some sayings about "disciples" (who may be regarded as the new Temple, Congregation,

---

[1] Jn ii. 21.   [2] 1 Chr. i. 1, 2 Chr. xxxvi. 23.   [3] Ezek. xlviii. 35.

Ecclesia, or Church—a word used by Matthew alone of the Evangelists). It is assumed, rather than expressed, by Matthew in the precept "tell it to the Church" and in the promise "Upon this rock will I build my Church[1]." Both in Matthew and in Mark Jesus does not go to the Temple till He goes to it before the last Passover which issues in His death.

In Luke, Jesus goes to the Temple, in some sense, thrice; first, as a babe, to be "presented to the Lord"; secondly, as a boy of twelve, to the Passover; thirdly, in manhood, as in Mark and Matthew, to the final Passover. The mention of these three visits undoubtedly has the effect of bringing before the Gentile reader the centralising influence of the Jewish Temple. But the picture of the second visit presents difficulties. It represents Jesus as "*sitting* in the midst of the doctors[2]." "*Sitting*," as the marginal reference shews, betokened a teacher. How incompatible such a posture with the thoughts called up in many of us by Holman Hunt's picture of "The Finding of Christ in the Temple"! That artist may be wrong. But at least some will feel his standing Jesus to be divinely natural. Doubtless, other artists have depicted the "sitting" Jesus of twelve years old in pictures of beauty—beauty in line and colour—but are they, and could they be, pictures of beauty in nature? The moral or spiritual difficulty raises the question whether Luke may not have confused this visit with one made in later years[3].

John, at all events, gives an entirely different impression in his account of Christ's first visit to the Temple. It differs, in tone, both from Luke and from Chronicles. It is not a visit of peace, but of war. Jesus goes up to the Passover, but it is not "the Passover of the Lord," but "the Passover of the Jews[4]." And He goes up "as a refiner's fire[5]." "The

---

[1] Mt. xviii. 17, xvi. 18. [2] Lk. ii. 46, comp. Mt. xxvi. 55.
[3] See pp. 94—5. [4] Jn ii. 13. [5] Mal. iii. 2.

71

Jews," with their polluted " Passover," are "destroying" the Temple, and Jesus bids them persist in their evil course if they wish to destroy it :—" Destroy this temple and in three days I will raise it up[1]."

Summing up the comparison of the Chronicler with the Evangelist, we may say that their attitudes, severally, to the Passover and the Temple, would suffice to indicate the deep gulf that divides the hyperbolic prosaist from the poet, the literal legalist from the disciple of the Spirit. But neither this nor other differences ought to make us forget that these two authors were probably alike, not only in being Jews, but also in conceiving it to be part of their duty to supply " omissions," severally, in writings that already had among Jews, and in writings that were soon to have among Christians, the authority of Scripture.

---

[1] Jn ii. 19. On the imperative see *Johannine Grammar* **2439** (iii)—(v).

CHAPTER VII

ORDER AND ARRANGEMENT IN HEBREW HISTORIES

§ 1. *Agreement between Kings and Chronicles*

THE last four Chapters of this Introduction will be devoted to an examination of the order and arrangement in the Four Gospels severally. This Chapter will prepare the way for them by inquiring into the order and arrangement in the Hebrew Historical Books, more particularly Kings[1] and Chronicles, just so far as to ask whether it can teach us anything about the very great differences in the order and arrangement adopted by some of the Evangelists.

Chronicles differs very slightly from Kings in its arrangement of parallel text. Its very large occasional insertions, and still larger and much more frequent omissions, do not prevent the Chronicler from retaining the same sequence as in the older work, that is to say, from following the order of the kings of Judah and Israel, reign by reign, but often condensing, or omitting, things relating to Israel as distinct from Judah. As for the order of things happening in each reign, where an important event is to be introduced, it is often marked off from what precedes by an introductory clause, such as "after these things." Only now and then are there slight deviations. The list of David's "mighty men" and their achievements is placed in the older work

---

[1] "Kings" includes "Samuel," see p. 15, n. 1.

73

as an appendix, after "the last words of David[1]," whereas
Chronicles gives them a place nearer to that which would
be appropriate for the account of their achievements[2]. But
such changes are rare. Almost invariably the Chronicler
adopts the old chronology.

Passing to the Gospels we recognise at once this great
difference, that in them there is as it were only one epoch,
or "reign"—that of Jesus; so that the only questions for
us are these two. First, do the Evangelists ever date the
birth and acts of the Messiah by the dates of any of the
"princes of this world," such as the Herods, or the Emperors
of Rome? Secondly, within the Messianic life, or "reign,"
do they use the Hebrew chronological linking clauses, "after
this" or "after these things," or do they by any other means
indicate short or long, definite or indefinite, intervals of
time?

These questions will come before us again, when we study
the order and arrangement in the several Gospels, but here
it will be convenient to make a few remarks on Hebrew
usage in Kings and Chronicles, and to shew how it might
affect the interpretation of our Gospels.

§ 2. *"After these things" in Hebrew*

The Hebrew for "after these *things*"—when "things"
is expressed by a separate noun—is literally "after these
words." When used for the first time, it introduces the
Promise to Abraham; when for the second, the Sacrifice
of Isaac[3]. In the second case the Jerusalem Targum supplies
some words, previously uttered, so as to make "after these
words" literally true. The ambiguity occasionable by the

---

[1] See 2 S. xxiii. 8 foll., following xxiii. 1 foll. "these be the last
words..."
[2] See 1 Chr. xi. 10 foll.
[3] Gen. xv. 1, xxii, 1.

twofold Hebrew meaning may be illustrated by such an expression as " *By the last words* of David the sons of Levi were numbered," where the margin has " *In the last acts*[1]." Of the thirteen instances in which the phrase is fully expressed, six are in Genesis[2].

Chronicles, with one exception (which concerns Hezekiah's reforms)[3] never writes " after *these things* " fully. Yet, under cover of the rendering " *acts*," the book is continually using the Hebrew " *words*"—mentioning, at the close of each reign, the *acts* of David, Solomon, Rehoboam, etc. Indeed the Hebrew title of the Book of Chronicles is "The *Acts* (lit. *Words*) of the Days," meaning "the acts of the king for the time being from day to day." In such a book, the natural course is to reserve the use of the word "acts" till the conclusion of each reign, and to denote the sequence of events during each reign by "after this," except in a special case such as the religious reformation of Hezekiah.

§ 3. " *After these things*," and " *after this*," in John

In John, " after these things " and " after this " occur more frequently than in any other book of the New Testament. For the most part, " after this " implies only a short interval[4]. But the radical distinction between the two is, perhaps, sometimes this, that " *after these things* "— whether the interval of time be short or long—implies a changed or new state of things, as in " *After these things* Joseph asked of Pilate that he might take away the body of

---

[1] 1 Chr. xxiii. 27.

[2] See Gesen. 183 *b*. In all these, "words" is expressed, but the form of the preposition sometimes slightly differs.

[3] Gesen. 183 *b* referring to 2 Chr. xxxii. 1 "after these *acts* (lit. *words*) and [deeds of] faithfulness" (where the parall. 2 K. xviii. 13 has "now in the fourteenth year of King Hezekiah"). Chron. has previously inserted two long chapters describing Hezekiah's acts of religious reformation. To these it refers as "*acts*."

[4] See *Johannine Grammar* 2394 and 2349 *a*.

Jesus[1]." Here "*these things*" were quite recently accomplished. But what great "*things*"!

Some thought of this kind—that is, of a changed condition of things, when the Jews entered on a course of "persecuting" Jesus—may perhaps explain another very difficult instance. It occurs in some of John's observations (about the ingratitude of the man healed by Jesus at the pool) which we may perhaps paraphrase thus :—"[*Some time*] *after these things* Jesus findeth him in the temple [Now, though he had gone into the temple to pray with his lips, he had never turned in his heart to Jesus, his Healer, but had returned to his old sins]. And Jesus said unto him, Behold, thou art made whole : no longer continue-sinning, lest a worse thing befall thee. The man went away and told the Jews that it was Jesus that had made him whole. And for this cause the Jews began-to-persecute Jesus, because he did these things on the sabbath[2]."

In Chronicles, the course of events, and the writer's feeling that he is describing the decline and fall of the House of Judah, ending in the destruction of the Temple, give a sad tone to the repetition of "after this." And that is the impression left by the last instance of the phrase, where there is a pathetic emphasis on "*all this*," describing the unhappy end of the last of the reformers : "*After all this*, when Josiah had prepared the temple, Neco king of Egypt went up...and Josiah went out against him...and hearkened not unto the words of Neco, from the mouth of God[3]." It is implied that there was a fatal blindness upon Josiah, even on this, the best of the later kings. Like the wicked Ahab—and with the same result—the pious Josiah "disguised himself...and hearkened not unto the words of Neco, from the mouth of God." Thus, dying, "lamented" by "all the singing men and singing women unto this day," he carried with him to the grave

---

[1] Jn xix. 38.   [2] Jn v. 14—16.   [3] 2 Chr. xxxv. 20.

Judah's last hope. And why? Because they had despised the words of God "until the wrath of the Lord arose against his people, and there was no remedy[1]."

In the Gospel, owing to an opposite course of events, and an opposite feeling in the writer, there is a note of joy and advance, not of sorrow and relapse, in the last use of the phrase under consideration : "*After these things* Jesus manifested himself again to the disciples at the sea of Tiberias[2]." A new condition of things is introduced wherein the disciples, refreshed by a morning meal ("come, break your fast") are to go forth to do the day's work for the Master, whether it be by "following" Him on the Way of the Cross or by "waiting" till He come.

§ 4. "*After these things,*" and "*after these words,*" in Luke

The only case where Luke uses "after these things" in Synoptic narrative[3] is as follows :—

Mk ii. 13–14	Mt. ix. 9	Lk. v. 27
And he went forth (*or,* out) again by the sea...and passing by he saw Levi the son of Alphaeus...	And Jesus, passing by thence, saw a man called Matthew...	And *after these things* he went forth (*or,* out) and beheld ...by name Levi...

Now what has just preceded is the healing of the paralysed man in the synagogue, so that Mark's "*went forth,*" or "*came out,*" without addition, might be explained, in the light of Matthew's "*thence,*" as meaning "*came out of the synagogue.*" But "*after these things*" (or, as the Diatessaron has it, "*after that*"), if interpreted as usual, would imply an interval (of long or short duration). The Diatessaron *repeats this story*

---

[1] 2 Chr. xxxv. 22—5, xxxvi. 16.   [2] Jn xxi. 1 foll.

[3] Luke uses it also in x. 1 "Now *after these things* the Lord appointed seventy others." But that is a tradition, not "Synoptic," but peculiar to Luke.

thrice, as referring to three distinct persons. In the first of these, to shew that the action followed immediately on the action in the synagogue, it inserts "[*out*] *of the synagogue.*" In the second, it inserts nothing. In the third and last, it retains a form of the Lucan phrase, "*after that*" :—

(i) Diatess. vi. 46 And when Jesus came out *of the synagogue* he saw a man sitting among the publicans named Matthew....

(ii) Diatess. vii. 9 And when he passed by [   ] he saw Levi the son of Alphaeus sitting among the tax-gatherers....

(iii) Diatess. vii. 25 And *after that*, Jesus went forth (*or*, came out) and saw a publican named Levi sitting among the publicans....

The Diatessaron apparently takes "*after that*" to denote an interval inconsistent with the supposition that the event to be described was identical with the one described by Mark as occurring when Jesus "*came out*," which it takes to mean "*came out of the synagogue.*"

There is other evidence of early confusion between the narratives of the calling of Levi, Matthew, Zacchaeus, and Nathanael[1]. Probably Luke intended, by this unique use of "*after these things*"—whether inserting it for clearness, or retaining it, contrary to his custom, for clearness—to imply an interval of some duration between what he had just related and what he goes on to relate. Diatessaron indirectly increases that probability.

This view might be supposed to be confirmed by a Lucan insertion in the Synoptic parallels in the Transfiguration, following Christ's words about "not tasting death" till the vision of "the Kingdom":—

---

[1] See *Son of Man* 3375 *k*.

Mk ix. 2	Mt. xvii. 1	Lk. ix. 28
And after six days Jesus taketh with him Peter...	And after six days Jesus taketh with him Peter...	Now it came to pass, *after these words*, about eight days, taking with him Peter...

But, as the number of "days" is expressed by all the Synoptists, Luke may have inserted "after these words" in order to shew that what he emphatically means is not "after *the events* I have been relating," but "after *these express ' words'* about a 'vision'—*words* that the reader will now find fulfilled[1]." In this instance, then, it cannot be inferred with certainty that Luke himself intends to suggest a revolutionising event, or a new condition of things, though perhaps that was in the mind of the author from whom he derives some of the features peculiar to his account of the Transfiguration.

§ 5. *"After" may sometimes mislead*

Mark says that "*after* John [the Baptist] was delivered up, Jesus came into Galilee preaching[2]." We naturally infer that He came *soon* "after." But take two parallel passages from Chronicles and the second Book of Samuel describing what happened *after* "David and all the people returned to Jerusalem." The reader will see below that the Chronicler jumps over the estrangement, revolt, and death, of Absalom. He covers about nine chapters of Samuel, in a single verse, and

---

[1] As regards Lk. "about *eight* days," it may be noted that Mark has μετὰ ἡμέρας but Matthew μεθ᾽ ἡμέρας, and μεθ᾽ in N.T. with accus. occurs elsewhere only in Jn xx. 26 "*after eight days*." "*Eight*," indicated by H, may have dropped out before the H in Mark's ἡμέρας, and "*six*" may be an error of Mark's followed by Matthew.

[2] Mk i. 14.

79

in the smoothest possible way, with the aid of the formula
"*after this*[1]."

The Chronicler is deliberately omitting. May not the
Evangelist (or the authority that he followed) be also deliberately omitting—not from a desire to curtail, but from
a want of special knowledge about anything except that part
of the gospel which Jesus preached at a particular time and
place? That is a question that will at all events have to be
considered.

Again, beside the danger of omission that might fail to
be noticed (arising from the free use of this chronological
formula) there is also that of transposition. In a history
written in episodes, many of which begin with "after these
things (*lit.* words)," some editors or translators might feel
less compunction (than in histories otherwise written) about
shifting the place of an episode, especially if "*after these
words*" occurred where no "words" had been mentioned.
Take, for example, "The king of Israel went to his house
heavy and displeased, and came to Samaria. And it came
to pass *after these words* that Naboth the Jezreelite had
a vineyard[2]." The LXX omits "*after these words*" and
places the twenty-first chapter (which is about Naboth's
vineyard) after the nineteenth chapter (which describes the
calling of Elisha by Elijah).

The reason for troubling the reader with this apparently
very unimportant detail is, that it may bear on a question

---

[1]   1 Chr. xx. 3—4.
...Jerusalem. *And it came to
pass after this* that there arose war
at Gezer with the Philistines.

2 S. xii. 31, xiii. 1, xv. 1, xxi. 18.
...Jerusalem. *And it came to
pass after this that* [Absalom had
a fair sister (xii. 31, xiii. 1)...*And
it came to pass after this that*
Absalom prepared (xv. 1)...*And it
came to pass after this that*] there
was again war with the Philistines
at Gob (xxi. 18).

[2] 1 K. xx. 43, xxi. 1.

by no means unimportant, the alleged disarrangement of some of the chapters of the Fourth Gospel. "*After these things*" comes at the beginning of its fifth, sixth, and seventh chapters. As long ago as the fourteenth century, a rearrangement of these chapters was suggested so as to place the sixth before the fifth[1]. And the Diatessaron places the sixth chapter, and almost all the fifth, before the greater part of the fourth. The facts alleged above appear—so far as concerns these chapters—to favour this arrangement, which must not be 'forgotten when we come to discuss passages taken from that portion of the Fourth Gospel.

---

[1] See *Disarrangements in the Fourth Gospel* p. 3, by F. Warburton Lewis B.A. (Cambridge: at the University Press, 1910). Some of his conclusions extend beyond the chapters above mentioned and do not seem to me so strong as the rest. The treatise does not (I think) refer to the use of the formula in Kings and Chronicles.

CHAPTER VIII

ORDER AND ARRANGEMENT IN MARK

§ 1. *Mark "did not write in order," if "order" includes*
"appropriate beginning and end"

PAPIAS makes the following statement :—" As for Mark, he
was Peter's interpreter and wrote accurately,...*but not in order*,
the things that were either said or done by Christ[1]." Perhaps
by the somewhat emphatic phrase "*either* said or done"
(instead of "said or done") Papias means that Mark wrote
down *either* Christ's acts *or else* His words, whichever happened to come before him in Peter's teaching or preaching
from day to day, without separating words from deeds in such
a way as to give a clear view of a progress of events, or a
progress in doctrine[2]. If so, we might freely paraphrase him
thus : "Mark might conceivably have now and then grouped
the words into a discourse, or a dialogue, of some length, but
he did not do so." This clause, whatever may be its precise
shade of meaning, need not detain us.

"Not in order," on the other hand, is at first sight
perplexing, especially in view of the fact that Matthew (whose
"order" Papias does not censure) generally follows the order
of Mark. It can be explained, however, from the accusations
(probably well known to Papias) brought against the history

---

[1] See *Enc. Bibl.* col. 1811 "Gospels."
[2] The same phrase, without "either," is used by Josephus *Contr.
Apion.* i. 10 (see below, p. 116, n. 2).

of Thucydides as being deficient in "order." They are recorded thus, by Dionysius of Halicarnassus early in the first century: "Now some find fault also with his *order*, since he has neither taken for his history the beginning that he ought to have taken, nor adjusted to it the end [that would have been] suitable; and they say that no small part of good arrangement consists in taking such a beginning as that nothing can [well] come before it, and in rounding off the action with such an end that nothing shall seem deficient in it[1]." In Dionysius, as in Papias, "order" is represented by the Greek *taxis*. It might mean "marshalling" or "arranging" of all the parts or members of a host. But it is technically applied to literary composition; and, in this sense, it appears to be used in the above-quoted criticism of Thucydides, with special reference, not to gradual development or ascent, nor to distinctions of subject-matter, but to rightness of "beginning" and of "end[2]."

Judged by this test, no well-known author fails so conspicuously as Mark. The "beginning" of his Gospel is— according to very early interpretations of Mark's ambiguous text—"John," who "came" and "baptized." Even if "John" were, when explained, a good beginning, it would hardly be so in a Gospel that does not explain who John was, and whence John came. This the Evangelist does not tell us. Indeed, he himself suggests—though the suggestion is only indirect— an earlier "beginning" than John, in the shape of a prophecy about John, by saying "even as it is written in Isaiah the prophet, Behold, I send...thy way." These words are not in Isaiah, but in Malachi. Mark's "beginning," then, is erroneous in its context as well as unsatisfactory in itself. The Greek critic would assuredly condemn it and ask how any advocate of Mark could say "Nothing could well come before 'John.'"

---

[1] Dionysius of Halicarnassus, *Judic. de Thucyd.* § 10.
[2] On the technical meaning of τάξις see Steph. *Thes.*, vol. vii, col. 1822.

Again, as to Mark's "end": no doubt if Papias could have been induced to accept as the genuine conclusion of Mark's Gospel the words in the spurious Mark-Appendix: "So then the Lord Jesus, after he had spoken to them, was received up into heaven and sat down at the right hand of God. And they went forth and preached everywhere, the Lord working with them, and confirming the word by the signs that followed. Amen"—he would have had to drop one half of his accusation. But a book of "good-tidings" that ends with "*they were afraid*" cannot be said to end appropriately. And if, as was almost certainly the case, his text of Mark ended with the words "And they went out and fled from the tomb...and they said nothing to any one, for *they were afraid*," then we can wonder no longer that—having the Greek literary sense of the word "order" in view—he declared that "Mark wrote accurately but *not in order*."

§ 2. *Mark is vague as to time and place*

Mark's first chronological phrase follows the Baptist's prediction, "he shall baptize you with the Holy Spirit," without any interval, thus: "And it came to pass *in those days* there came Jesus from (*or*, of) Nazareth of Galilee, and was baptized...[1]." This is a type of Mark's general chronological vagueness. When we come to consider this passage in its order, we shall find that the parallel Matthew ("came *to be* baptized") suggests that Jesus may have *come to John* (perhaps to hear his teaching) some time before *coming to John to be baptized*. Also the parallel Luke implies that John, before the arrival of Jesus, had baptized great multitudes ("*when all the people had been baptized*, Jesus also having been baptized and being [now] in the act of praying..."). But Mark does not suggest or imply anything of the kind.

---

[1] Mk i. 9, parallel to Mt. iii. 13, Lk. iii. 21.

Mark's topography is equally vague. He tells us indeed that John was baptizing "in the wilderness." But in what wilderness? Not assuredly in "the wilderness" mentioned in his preceding sentence "the voice of one crying *in the wilderness*"; for that refers to the "wilderness" travelled over by the Israelites returning from Babylon to their native land. Matthew defines John's wilderness as "the wilderness *of Judaea.*" But, as far as Mark is concerned, we are left in ignorance. And, as we shall see, Luke does not appear to accept Matthew's definition. The same charge of vagueness as to locality extends to the words "*from* (or, *of*) Nazareth." We do not know—and it will be shewn hereafter that we have no means of knowing with absolute certainty—whether it means that Jesus *of* Nazareth, wherever He might happen to be, came and was baptized by John, or that Jesus came to John straight *from* Nazareth.

It has been shewn, above, that one instance of Mark's use of "went out," when applied to Jesus, caused ambiguity, because he did not tell us whence Jesus "went out[1]." We were left in doubt about time as well as about place, not knowing whether Jesus "went out" *at once* from the place last mentioned, namely, the synagogue, or "went out [of doors]" *later on*, upon some new journey. Ambiguity might also arise from a doubt whether the "going out" was customary, or a single act—perhaps a final act.

Thus, in the only passage where the three Synoptists agree in saying that Jesus, or Jesus and His disciples, "*went out to the Mount of Olives*," Luke adds "he went-his-way according to the custom[2]." On the other hand in a narrative in which Mark and Luke make it clear that Jesus *used regularly* to go outside the City to Bethany, or to the Mount of Olives, Matthew says "*Abandoning them*, he went out of

---

[1] See pp. 77—8.
[2] Mk xiv. 26, Mt. xxvi. 30 "*they went out*," Lk. xxii. 39 "and *having gone out* (ἐξελθών) he went-his-way (ἐπορεύθη) according to the custom."

85

the city "—using language that would naturally mean a final departure from the City[1].

Perhaps the most interesting instance of varying tradition about Christ "going out" is connected with the following, where Luke omits the word :—

Mk xiii. 1–2	Mt. xxiv. 1–2	Lk. xxi. 5–6
And as he was *going-out-on-his-way*[2] out of the temple, one of his disciples saith unto him, Teacher, see! What stones! And what buildings! And Jesus said to him, Seest thou...	And Jesus, *having gone-out*[2] away-from the temple, was going-on-his-way, and his disciples came-to him to shew him the buildings of the temple. But he answered and said unto them, See ye not...	And as some were saying concerning the temple (lit.) that 'It is adorned with beautiful stones and offerings,' he said, These things, which ye behold...

Here follows, in all the Synoptists, the prediction "There shall not be left stone upon stone." Then, in Mark and Matthew, it is said that Jesus was "sitting on the Mount of Olives" and was "privately" questioned, "When shall these things be?" Mark says the questioners were Peter, James, John and Andrew. Matthew says they were "the disciples." Luke, who mentions "questioning," but omits "Mount of Olives" and "privately," has "they-questioned," no pronoun being added. Hence Luke's "they" may refer to Luke's preceding "some."

These small details deserve the closest attention in view of the exaggerated importance attached by many modern critics to the Synoptic reports of Christ's sayings, at this point, concerning the Last Days. They are attributed indeed by all

---

[1] See Origen (Lomm. iv. 71 foll.) and Jerome, on Mt. xxi. 17 καταλιπών, parall. to Mk xi. 19, Lk. xxi. 37. The context shews that Matthew does not attach this meaning to "abandon." But he may have taken it from some narrative where it referred either (1) to a final departure, or (2) to a departure with a sense of reprobation ("giving them up [as hopeless]").

[2] Mk ἐκπορευομένου ἐκ..., Mt. ἐξελθὼν ἀπό...

the Synoptists to Jesus, but, as the reader perceives, amid different audiences, and in different circumstances. In the predictions themselves also Luke deviates widely from Mark and Matthew. Later on they will claim discussion in their place. But it may be well to note here at once, that, by the rule of Johannine intervention, since Luke is silent, John is bound to intervene.

It can be shewn (I believe) that he does intervene. And surely the occasion was one that called on the latest Evangelist to tell the Church all that he knew. It could not but be a most interesting question in the first century, and especially shortly after the fall of Jerusalem, "What were the precise words of Jesus about the destruction of the Temple, and when, and where, and to whom, were they uttered? When precisely did Jesus for the very last time *go-out-from*, or *abandon*, the Temple, or the City, and leave it to its fate? With what utterance did He depart? Are we to regard Him as *going out* only once and in the literal sense? Or did He *go out* as a martyr[1]? Or as a mediator? Or in all these senses?" It will appear (I believe) that John answers, in effect, "In all these senses[2]."

On one or two occasions the Marcan "going out" is said, or implied, to be from a "boat." And this leads us to observe that Mark, in describing the acts of Jesus, mentions "the sea," in his short Gospel, sixteen or seventeen times, as compared with ten or eleven times in Matthew and none in Luke[3]. The reason may lie partly perhaps in early Petrine reminiscences of Peter's boat. These, peculiarly interesting once in the primitive Galilaean gospel, may have remained in the earliest

---

[1] Comp. Heb. xiii. 13 "Let us *go-out* to him, outside the camp."

[2] Jn xviii. 1 literally; xviii. 4 to intercede for the disciples (*ib.* 8) "let these depart," and xix. 5 as the mediating Man of Sorrows; xix. 17 as the Martyr, "bearing his own cross."

[3] On Luke's avoidance of the word "sea," applied to what he calls the "*lake* of Gennesaret," see *Johannine Grammar* **2045**.

of the now extant written gospels, beyond the days when such details had lost much of their interest—lost it, at least, except so far as they had passed into poetic history and gained a new interest by becoming symbolically attractive, when the boat symbolized the Church.

But this raises the question, " How soon did some of these things pass into poetry ? " The first two verses of Mark's Gospel, quoting prophecy, warn us that he may have prophecies in view later on, even when he does not quote them. There can hardly be a doubt, for example, that in mentioning the early gospel in Galilee, he would *think*, though he does not actually speak, about that prophecy concerning " *Galilee* " and "the *way of the sea*" which Matthew quotes in full just before the words " From that time Jesus began to preach[1]."

If the primitive traditions followed by Mark, when they mentioned " Galilee," had prophecy about Galilee in view, although they did not quote prophecies, then it becomes more easy to understand that those same primitive traditions, when they spoke about the " boat " and the " sea," may sometimes have had Christian hymns in view, although they do not quote hymns[2].

§ 3. *Indications of Marcan omission*

Mark's vagueness in chronology leaves it open to believe that, like the Chronicler[3], he may have made deliberate omissions. The Chronicler makes them in order to subordinate Israel to Judah. The Evangelist may make them because he prefers to say nothing at all about things in Judaea of which he has no detailed information. We have seen above that he says "After John was delivered-up,

---

[1] Mt. iv. 15—17, quoting Is. ix. 1.

[2] *E.g.* Jn vi. 21 suggests a Christian application of Ps. cvii. 30 " and so he bringeth them unto the haven of their desire."

[3] See pp. 55 foll., 58 foll., 79 foll.

Jesus came into Galilee[1]," but he does not say *how long* "*after*," nor *whence* Jesus came. Later on, he says, using a phrase unique in the New Testament, "he entered into Capernaum *after-an-interval-of days*[2]." When this expression occurs in Hebrew, "days" is rendered by the Targum "an appointed-time of days," and there the context implies at all events more than two or three days[3]. Still later, Mark says simply "he went forth again," where, as has been said, Luke implies an interval of some duration by inserting "*after these things*[4]."

A little later—and again without mention of interval—Mark describes Jesus as going on the sabbath "through the cornfields." This phrase, taken with its context, gives us at last something approaching to a date. For the mention of "cornfields" in which the disciples "pluck the ears of corn" indicates a date not very long after the Passover. The beginning of the harvest season was celebrated during the feast of unleavened bread, by waving before the Lord a sheaf of the firstfruits of the harvest; and the Feast of Weeks, celebrating the conclusion of the wheat harvest, fell on the fiftieth day after the waving. These facts lead us to ask where, in Mark's Gospel, we are to place the Passover that preceded this "plucking the ears of corn." (1) Did that Passover fall between Christ's Temptation and His coming "into Galilee preaching the gospel of God[5]," and has Mark omitted it without warning us of the omission? Or (2) did

---

[1] Mk i. 14.

[2] Mk ii. 1 δι' ἡμερῶν. Note the parall. Lk. v. 17 "and it came to pass *in one of the days.*"

[3] Judg. xi. 4, xiv. 8, xv. 1. In the last two instances, the interval is long enough to allow (1) the deposit of a honeycomb in the body of a slaughtered lion, (2) the re-marriage of Samson's wife.

[4] See above, p. 78.

[5] This, as will be seen later on, resembles John's view. In that case there must be a long interval between Mk i. 13 "and the angels ministered unto him" and Mk i. 14 "Now after John was delivered up, Jesus came..."

it fall just before Christ's baptism, so that it just escaped coming within the whole of the period included in Mark's Gospel—which period would then be almost exactly one year, beginning a day or two after a first Passover, and ending on a second Passover, the day of, or the day before, the Crucifixion?

Of these two views, the second appears incompatible with Mark's own subsequent mention of "cornfields." For suppose a Passover to have just preceded Christ's Baptism. After the Baptism follow forty days of the Temptation, making six weeks at the very least from the Passover. Then comes the first preaching in Galilee, and the call of the fishermen, and the exorcism in the synagogue of Capernaum, followed by acts of healing[1]; then, a journey "throughout all Galilee," during which the crowds, drawn by His "preaching and casting out devils," prevented Him from openly "entering into a city[2]." The interval between the beginning of this journey and the return to Capernaum is the one—and, according to Old Testament precedent, not a short one—implied in the phrase "*after an interval of days*[3]." For these two courses of preaching we can hardly allow less than a month. Probably much more should be allowed; but a month, added to the above-mentioned six weeks and odd days, makes at least ten or eleven weeks from our initial Passover. Long before this the harvest—wheat as well as barley—would have been gathered in, and there would have been no "ears of corn" for the disciples to "pluck."

These facts indicate that there is more to be said than appears on the surface, for the first of the two views above mentioned. That view would be compatible with the Johannine Gospel, which inserts an early visit of Jesus to the Temple during a Passover, and before the Baptist's imprisonment.

Here it is natural to pause and ask whether we can find

---

[1] Mk i. 14—38.   [2] Mk i. 39—45.   [3] See p. 89, n. 3.

in Mark, or in any of the Synoptists, any trace whatever of a second visit of Christ's to the Temple, so that we might say " There is some evidence to shew that there were more visits than one. John has recorded them in detail. The Synoptists have omitted all but the last ; but, in their records of the last, they have left discrepancies, and perhaps duplications, which may be faint reminiscences—not understood by the Synoptists themselves—of a second visit (or perhaps a third, too) of which—as being outside his province, and not well known to him—Mark has recorded nothing, except in such a form as to escape notice"?

We may exclaim, "How could the Evangelists fail to know? Was it not their duty to know?" Such a question would betoken our own ignorance—ignorance of that which the Evangelists would consider their "duty" in the first years of the Church, up to the time, say, of the fall of Jerusalem. The Christians of those days were highly practical men, and were mainly concerned with Christ in three aspects, first, as the Giver of promises of salvation which could be obtained by "belief" and by the performance of His precepts; secondly, as the Lord from heaven, who might "come" at any moment to establish His Kingdom on earth; thirdly, as the Fulfiller of prophecies in such a way that He not only enabled them to believe, but also gave them power to "mightily confute" their adversaries[1]. Mere anecdotes about Christ's journeyings and actions would find little place in early and compendious handbooks of the first Christian missionaries. They might be looked down upon as treating of Christ "in the flesh" or even "after the flesh[2]," until Luke came to broaden the conception of evangelistic "duty." In a Galilaean compendium dealing with the gospel in Galilee and the north, it is conceivable that two or three visits of warning to Jerusalem might be at first grouped together for convenience and afterwards confused as one.

---

[1] Acts xviii. 28.   [2] 2 Cor. v. 16.

If there has been such confusion, the place in which traces of it are to be first looked for is manifestly the Synoptic account of the Purification of the Temple, in which we must search for signs of duplication suggesting *two* visits such as might be described in two documents, each beginning with the words "And Jesus went to Jerusalem. And he entered into the Temple and...." There are no such traces in Matthew, except that, following Mark, he inserts in one passage the statement "*went into Jerusalem*" where the parallel Luke omits it[1]. But Mark, in the same passage, adds several words: "And he went into Jerusalem, *into the Temple, and, having looked-round-on all things, the hour being now late, he went-forth to Bethany with the twelve.*" This seems to oscillate between two meanings. Mark might have described something like a visit of inspection in which Jesus might have delayed resorting to extreme measures because He wished to consider what should be done, or because He wished to give the offenders time to mend their ways. But "the hour being now late" suggests something quite different: "He would have done more, but He could not. He was prevented by the sunset." It is not surprising that Luke omits this, and that the parallel Matthew has something quite different[2].

At this point, in weighing the evidence, there comes in for consideration the question how much or how little importance we are to attach to the rule of Johannine Intervention. For according to that rule, John is bound to intervene, since Mark has a perplexing insertion, which Matthew completely alters, and Luke altogether omits. We cannot explain the alteration or the omission on the ground that the context has to do with the Baptist or Elijah, or with

---

[1] Mk xi. 11, Mt. xxi. 10, om. by Lk. xix. 38 foll.

[2] Mt. xxi. 10—11 "And when he was come into Jerusalem, all the city was stirred, saying, Who is this? And the multitudes said, This is the prophet Jesus, from Nazareth of Galilee."

Herods or lepers, or with any other subject excluded from the Johannine Gospel. There is no way of escaping one of two conclusions. Either (1) the rule of Johannine Intervention fails here, or (2) John somewhere intervenes to describe something that corresponds to what Mark here inserts and Matthew and Luke alter or omit.

Many readers will probably prefer the former conclusion. Not unnaturally—at present. Yet, when the whole of the Marcan narrative is examined in its order, some of them will perhaps change their minds. The additional instances that will have come before them of Johannine Intervention, and the further internal evidence of the Marcan story of the Purification of the Temple, as compared with that of Matthew —shewing curious Marcan insertions and apparent transpositions—will produce in many (I believe) a conviction, beyond that which can be expected to be produced by the evidence at present before them, that Mark, in his Withering of the Fig-tree and its context, has preserved a confused and futile account of a preliminary visit to the Temple, about which, knowing no details as to what was done, he inferred that nothing was done. He inferred also that, since Jesus must have *seen* what was going on, and did nothing, the visit was to be regarded as, in effect, one of inspection, "*looking round*[1]." Then he added another inference, that the reason

---

[1] Mk xi. 11. "Looking round," περιβλεψάμενος, in the traditions of which Mark took notes, might mean (1) literally, a turning round of the whole body, such as was ascribed (*Buddhist Suttas*, p. 64) to the Buddha ; (2) a mystical act of the Saviour, who "*looked round*" like Moses (Exod. ii. 12 περιβλεψάμενος, on which see Philo, and comp. Is. lix. 16) and saw none but Himself to save Israel. The Greek word had many meanings and was liable to confusion. Comp. Epictet. iii. 14. 3 περίβλεψαι, ἐνσείσθητι. Also note Mk xi. 11 περιβλεψάμενος parall. to Mt. xxi. 10 ἐσείσθη, and Mk xv. 11 ἀνέσεισαν (v.r. ἔπεισαν) parall. to Mt. xxvii. 20 ἔπεισαν, and comp. Lk. xxiii. 5 ἀνασείει—all betokening conflicting Greek traditions. Mark's use of περιβλέπομαι will come before us in its order. It occurs nowhere in N.T. except Mark, six times (and Lk. vi. 10 copying Mk iii. 5).

for doing nothing was that "*it was late.*" All this Matthew alters, and Luke omits[1].

But Luke may be said to compensate in some sort elsewhere. Like John, he relates an earlier visit of Jesus to the Temple, but unlike John, a visit of peace not of war. In this, Luke represents Jesus as saying to His parents, " *What [is it] that ye sought me [for]* " ? and then, " Knew ye not that I must needs be in the [*business,* or, *place*] of my Father[2] ? " After this Jesus "*goes down*" with them to Nazareth. Much of this has a Johannine sound. (1) The first words of Jesus in Luke are almost identical with His first words in John "*What seek ye*[3]? " (2) In Luke, Jesus very seldom speaks of God as "*my Father*[4]," but in John the phrase is frequent. (3) In the Johannine account of the Purification of the Temple, Jesus calls it " *my Father's house*[5]." (4) In John, just before (not after) the first visit to the Temple, it is said that Jesus "*went down*" with His mother and His brethren to Capernaum[6].

If there has been here any borrowing on the part of Luke or John from a common source, it seems more probable that Luke, than that John, gave the traditions a wrong interpretation. If Luke was wrong, the explanation would seem to be that he found in existence an undated Marcan tradition that Jesus on some occasion preceding the actual Purification of the Temple came to Jerusalem[7], and went into the Temple,

---

[1] Mk xi. 11, Mt. xxi. 10—11, Lk. xix. 38 foll.

[2] Lk. ii. 49. [3] Jn i. 38.

[4] It occurs in Lk. x. 22 (parall. to Mt. xi. 27) and xxii. 29, xxiv. 49, both peculiar to Luke. The question of the original Aramaic expressions for Christ's appellations of God is a very complicated one (see *Son of Man,* Index, " Father ").

[5] Jn ii. 16. [6] Jn ii. 12.

[7] Mk xi. 15 "and *they come to Jerusalem,*" xi. 27 "and *they come again to Jerusalem,*" have no parallels in Matthew or Luke. Taken with xi. 11 "and he *entered into Jerusalem,*" they constitute a threefold Marcan mention of visiting Jerusalem, which is perhaps to be regarded as intentional and allusive, representing a threefold warning. See p. 28, n. 3.

and "looked round" without doing anything. This or parts of this he may have blended with another tradition, that Jesus, in quite early days, held a discussion with the Jews in the Temple, and that He called the Temple "my Father's [house]."

In concluding these observations about Mark we may do well to note that, as he thrice mentions "*coming to Jerusalem*," so also he thrice mentions "*coming to Capernaum*[1]"; and perhaps, as regards both places, it was intended, in the original poetic tradition, to convey that both cities received a threefold warning from the Messiah. Also we must remark that either Jesus was very lax in attending the three Feasts at Jerusalem, as enjoined by the Law, or else the Synoptists have been very reticent. Even though they were silent as to the details of the two other Feasts, we might have expected that they would mention the fact that He went up to Jerusalem on two other occasions before His last visit. But there is no such mention—unless we can extract one, as suggested above, from Mark.

It must be confessed that if we accept as historical the Johannine account of an early purification of the Temple, occurring before John the Baptist was imprisoned, we raise two new and difficult questions. First, why was not John the Baptist found standing by the side of Jesus, at the first Passover, encouraging and aiding Him in His attempt to purify the Temple? Was it because, for some reason or other, the Baptist deliberately absented himself from the Paschal sacrifice? Surely it could not be that, though present, he took no share in the attempt to purify the House of God[2]. Secondly, why does the Fourth Gospel

---

[1] Mk i. 21, ii. 1, ix. 33, with two or three parallels in Matthew, but not in Luke except as to the first (Lk. iv. 31).

[2] See *Son of Man* 3584 *b* on the "incompatibility (διαφορότης)" between the purificatory rites of the Essenes and those of the Temple, to which they sent offerings, but which they did not attend, "performing

make no mention of subsequent attempts of Jesus to purify the Temple, either at the last Passover (when the Synoptists mention such attempts) or at any intervening one between the first and the last? Is it because the Evangelist assumes that at each visit these attempts of Jesus were renewed? To neither of these questions do I know any satisfactory answer.

These difficult hypotheses, however, are not so startling as the facts—not hypotheses but facts—which stare us in the face in Mark's erroneous beginning, and truncated end. Who could have supposed that this error and this truncation would be so far tolerated in the first written Christian Gospel that they have actually come down to our days, instead of being amended so completely and universally as to be buried in oblivion before the first century was over?

Some of this difficulty would be diminished if we could confirm by evidence the antecedent probability that Mark, like Thucydides, left his history unfinished. He may have written under pressure, and away from books, in prison, perhaps, with nothing but rough notes and memory to rely on. Perhaps the ink was not dry in the final words " for they were afraid," when he was summoned to execution. Nevertheless, suppose what we will, it must always remain one of the most painful paradoxes of literature—to say nothing of religion—that a work of such worldwide importance should have been composed by an author who so manifestly did not write, and did not try to write, in what an educated Greek would describe as "order."

---

their sacrifices by their own selves (ἐφ' ἑαυτῶν)." Was John an Essene? If so, how could he, at first, have been favoured by the Pharisees? Perhaps John was an instance of the latitude often allowed to a prophet— spontaneously by the people, and unwillingly by their rulers, who were constrained for a time to follow the popular mood.

CHAPTER IX

ORDER AND ARRANGEMENT IN MATTHEW

§ 1. *Matthew has an appropriate "beginning" and "end"*

PASSING to the subject of the "order" in Matthew, we will consider it first from the point of view of those critics, above referred to, who declared that "order" required an appropriate beginning and end. Matthew begins with Abraham : "The book of the generation of Jesus Christ, the son of David, the son of *Abraham*." He ends with the saying of Jesus, "*I am with you* alway, even unto the consummation of the age (lit. *aeon*)." The son and the grandson of Abraham —to whom God had promised Himself in the words "I am thy shield and thy exceeding great reward[1]"—were the special recipients of a promise to be "*with*" *them*. Both to Isaac, and to Jacob, He had said "*I am with thee*[2]." Matthew (and Matthew alone) records, as a title of the Messiah, "Immanuel," "God *with us*[3]." Matthew also alone contains the words "Where two or three are gathered together in my name, *there am I in the midst of them*[4]."

Abraham, according to Isaiah, was the "rock" from which the nation of Israel was hewn. A Jewish tradition declared that, until he came, the Lord could not begin to build up a people for Himself[5]. All was swamp. When Abraham came, then God, Himself the Rock of Salvation, discerned in him

---

[1] Gen. xv. 1.
[2] Gen. xxvi. 24, xxviii. 15.
[3] Mt. i. 23 quoting Is. vii. 14.
[4] Mt. xviii. 20.
[5] See *Son of Man* 3595—6.

something of His own divine steadfastness and truth, and made Himself the Patriarch's " exceeding great reward," and became an " Immanuel " to his descendants:—that is Matthew's theory, and it pervades his Gospel. He alone mentions the " church " or " congregation[1]." He alone mentions the " rock " on which it is to be built[2].

These thoughts, if pursued, would lead us on to the middle of Matthew's Gospel. But our present business is rather with its beginning and its end ; and we maintain that, from Matthew's point of view, they are appropriate. He writes about an " *aeon*." Its " consummation " is mentioned in his last verse. Its beginning is implied in his first verse, " the son of Abraham," meaning the spiritual Son of Abraham, the Son of God's Promise to Abraham, in whom " all the nations of the world " were to be " blessed." For Abraham the Lord was able to " raise up sons," even " from stones[3]." The gathering or raising up of these " stones " is to be the work of Christ through His apostles—that " building up " on which Paul constantly insists (though we sometimes miss it because it hides itself in our Authorised Version under the mask of " edifying "), and on which the Petrine Epistle with its emphasis on the " living stones " is still more directly insistent. Matthew does not write about those further aeons into which the reign of the Messiah will extend[4]. He limits his Gospel to that particular aeon which began with the coming of the promised Messiah. He came to build up that Church which the Pharisees—" daubers of the wall[5]," not " builders of the wall "—had failed to build. His Gospel ends with the sending forth of the builders to build in the name of " Jesus Christ, the son of David, the son of Abraham[6]," and to build on that

---

[1] Mt. xvi. 18, xviii. 17.   [2] Mt. xvi. 18.   [3] Mt. iii. 9, Lk. iii. 8.

[4] For the plural use of *aeon*, compare Lk. i. 33 "he shall reign over the house of Jacob unto the *aeons*."

[5] " Daubers of the Wall," a name given to the Pharisees in a *Zadokite Fragment*, on which see *Light on the Gospel* 3996 *a* foll.

[6] Mt. i. 1.

Rock of which Abraham was the type and Jesus was the fulfilment. Building on that Rock they would have His presence always with them "unto the consummation of *the aeon*[1]."

§ 2. *Matthew "wrote in order," of a kind, but not chronological "order"*

At the conclusion of the Sermon on the Mount, Matthew says "*And it came to pass, when Jesus made-an-end-of* these words, the multitudes were astonished..."; and at the conclusion of the precepts to the Twelve, Matthew says "*And it came to pass, when Jesus made-an-end-of* giving commandments to his twelve disciples, he passed-away thence to teach and preach in their cities[2]." Now in the Sermon on the Mount Matthew has collected a multitude of precepts, all bearing on the New Law. Internal evidence indicates that these were not all uttered at one time or at so early a time. External evidence to the same effect comes from Luke, who places several of these sayings much later, adding the occasions on which they were uttered. Again, in the Precepts to the Twelve, Matthew combines, along with a version of Mark's Precepts to the Twelve, several precepts not in Mark. Many of these shew internal signs of a later date. And once more the evidence of Luke confirms the internal evidence. Luke places them in a separate document, the Precepts to the Seventy.

These two instances suggest that the use of the clause "and it came to pass when Jesus *had made-an-end*" may resemble that of the clause "after these things," which, as we found above, served—in Kings and Chronicles—to close one epoch or one important narrative, so as to introduce another. Somewhat similarly, "*made-an-end*" is used in Genesis to conclude (1) God's promise to Abraham, of a covenant with

---

[1] Mt. xxviii. 20.   [2] Mt. vii. 28, xi. 1.

Isaac, (2) Isaac's blessing of Jacob, (3) Jacob's blessing of the twelve patriarchs[1].

Matthew's long formula, or refrain, is used five times in all, often preceding a mention of change of place as well as of subject[2]. The refrain thrice mentions "words," once "parables," and once "giving-precepts." "Words" applies to the Sermon on the Mount, which, besides being a blessing (beginning "Blessed are the poor") is also a Law like that of which it is said that Moses "*made-an-end-of* speaking all these words to all Israel[3]."

There is evidence indicating that this refrain did not proceed from the author—whoever he may have been— of the Greek text of our Matthew. For, as has been acutely observed, "There is nothing distinctively Matthaean in *it-came-to-pass*"; on the contrary, "followed by a finite verb, it is only found in these five places in Matthew, while it occurs twenty-two times in Luke (also twice in Mark and nowhere else in N.T.)[4]." Moreover an arrangement in five books is found in the Psalms as well as in the Pentateuch, in the Aboth, and in other writings of Jewish origin before, or shortly after, the Christian era[5]. This points to the conclusion that Matthew's Gospel is of a composite character. But we are concerned rather with the order of the Gospel as it stands, than with the nature and the sources of its contents. Examining the present text, we conclude that the ultimate author or editor has handed down to us a history in which order of time has been subordinated to order of subject.

---

[1] Gen. xvii. 22, xxvii. 30 (but not after xxvii. 40 at the conclusion of the blessing of Esau), xlix. 33. It is also used of God in Gen. ii. 2 (ending work) and xviii. 33 "*made-an-end-of* communing with Abraham"; and of Moses in Deut. xxxii. 45 "*made-an-end-of* speaking all these words to all Israel." See Mandelkern, pp. 560—1.

[2] The five instances are in vii. 28, xi. 1, xiii. 53, xix. 1, xxvi. 1.

[3] Deut. xxxii. 45.

[4] See *Horae Synopticae*, p. 165 for details.   [5] *Ib.* p. 164.

Where the system of grouping does not stand in the way, and especially near the end of the Gospel—where "words" fall into the background and long discourses are non-existent —Matthew follows Mark's order, as regards the acts of Christ. But in the earlier part he sacrifices Mark's chronology (as in the case of the above-mentioned breach of the sabbath in the cornfields) for the sake of grouping sayings together in accordance with their subject-matter. In defence of Matthew it may be urged that we find something like his system practised on one occasion in Exodus, where nothing is recorded except a law inflicting death for labouring on the sabbath, whereas Numbers, along with the law, records the facts that gave rise to the law[1]. What Exodus is to Numbers, that (it may be argued) Matthew is, in some cases, to Luke, as regards the utterances of Christ. But it will be shewn in the next section that Matthew sometimes does more than omit circumstances and transpose utterances.

§ 3. *Matthew's arrangement of evidence*

Of all the evidence for the Messianic claims of Jesus the most powerful—after the power of the personality of Jesus Himself had ceased to be exerted on earth—appears to have been that which was derived from prophecy. By "evidence" we here mean appeal to the reason, not to the heart. And we infer the strength of the appeal to prophecy, partly from what may be implied as to the earliest traditions of Christian preaching and controversy from the writings of Barnabas and Justin, but principally from the first-century evidence as to the cogency of the arguments of Peter, Paul, and Apollos, contained in the Epistles as well as in the Acts[2]. How Matthew

---

[1] Numb. xv. 32—6, Exod. xxxv. 2—3, xxxi. 14—15.
[2] Comp. Acts xviii. 28 on Apollos, "He mightily confuted the Jews, publicly shewing *by the scriptures* that Jesus was the Christ."

dealt with prophecy we may better consider after a word or two on Mark's employment of it.

Perhaps we ought rather to say "Mark's non-employment of it." For after quoting, in his own person, and in the first two verses of his Gospel, a prophecy from Malachi, and another from Isaiah, both of which he attributes to Isaiah, Mark never quotes prophecy again. When he uses the expressions "came into Galilee" and "by the sea of Galilee" at the beginning of Christ's preaching, we may think it probable that he is alluding to Isaiah's prophecy "by the way of the sea, Galilee"; and when he describes Jesus as "riding on an ass," we may feel it to be absolutely certain that he has "it was prophesied" *in his mind*; but he does not write the formula with his pen[1]. Jesus, in Mark, quotes "scripture," but even Jesus (in Mark) never quotes it formally as from a "prophet." Mark, in his own person—after his introductory error about the prophet Isaiah—never mentions either "scripture" or "prophet."

Very different is the course adopted by Matthew. He, when he sees fulfilments of Scripture in the acts of Christ, frankly quotes the very words, and often tells us that the act came to pass "*in order that*" they "*might be fulfilled.*" Thus, in the parallels to the instances of Marcan silence just mentioned ("came into Galilee" and the "riding on an ass") where Mark narrates the events without the prophecy, Matthew narrates the events as *coming to pass* "*in order that*" the prophecy "*might be fulfilled*[2]."

In these two instances we owe Matthew nothing but thanks for supplying what Mark apparently implies. But when Matthew on his own account—that is to say, without a parallel either in Mark or Luke—introduces a detail or event that (he says) "*came to pass in order that so-and-so might be fulfilled,*" a doubt arises. And that this doubt was utilised

---

[1] Mk i. 14, 16, xi. 7.　　　[2] Mt. iv. 12—16, xxi. 3—7.

by hostile critics of Matthew's Gospel at an early date is indicated by Jerome[1], who, after quoting several passages from the New Testament—almost all from Matthew—says that he refers to them and to their different renderings simply to defend his own method of translating, and "not to convict the evangelists of falsification—a charge worthy only of impious men like Celsus, Porphyry, and Julian."

This, taken with the context, indicates that some critics had accused Matthew of error in connection with some of these prophecies. For example, in connection with the prophecy about the "ass," Mark and Luke, *not quoting any prophecy*, speak of only one animal; Matthew, *quoting the prophecy about "an ass, and a colt the foal of an ass,"* mentions two animals; John, *quoting only part of the prophecy, a part that mentions only one animal*, himself mentions only one. It is difficult to doubt that Matthew, in quoting the prophecy about the two animals, has assumed the existence of two, and that the assumption was incorrect[2].

Now it has always been a historical difficulty for those who desire to take the most favourable view of the accuracy of Matthew's Gospel, that no other Evangelist mentions some of the events which he alone introduces, and introduces as "fulfilling" Scripture. Among these are the flight of Christ's parents into Egypt, and the subsequent recall from Egypt, "fulfilling" Hosea's prophecy "out of Egypt have I called my son[3]." Another is the massacre of the innocents, recorded

---

[1] See Jerome's *Letters* lvii. (transl. p. 115 foll.) quoting Mt. xxvi. 31, ii. 13—15, ii. 23, i. 22—3.

[2] In his commentary on Mt. xxi. 4, Jerome admitted that "according to the letter, in so short a journey, He could not have sat on both animals ...Therefore since [the literal] history implies something impossible or unbecoming, we are transported [by it] to higher things," that is, to allegory. Mt. xxi. 2 and 7 are both so adapted as to refer to two animals, differing therein from the closely parallel Mark.

[3] Hos. xi. 1. The Pharisaic Ebionites, in their version of Matthew, which they termed "the Gospel according to the Hebrews," omitted the first two chapters.

by Matthew alone and connected by him with the weeping of Rachel for her children mentioned by Jeremiah[1].

Josephus makes no mention of such a massacre. Nor does Luke. No reason can be given why Luke should have omitted it if he had believed it to be historical. It would have magnified God's Providence. Nor would it have interfered with his view, namely, that Jesus was born at Bethlehem by a kind of providential accident, instead of being born at Nazareth. No historian, outside the Christian Church, mentions the massacre, till the fifth century; and Matthew's general habit of quoting prophecy, when he records traditions of fulfilment mentioned by no other Evangelist, necessarily throws doubt on the authenticity of all of them[2].

Matthew's attitude—and indeed the Jewish attitude generally—toward historical evidence may be illustrated by his refrain of "fourteen generations" in the genealogy of Jesus, concerning which Horae Hebraicae says, "Although all things do not square exactly in this threefold number of *fourteen generations*, yet there is no reason why this should be charged as a fault upon Matthew, when in the Jewish schools themselves it obtained for a custom, yea, almost for an axiom, to reduce things and numbers to the very same, when they were near alike[3]." The author then quotes, from "a hundred examples," a statement in the Mishna that five things happened "on the ninth day of the month Ab," and adds "Not that they believed all these things fell out precisely the same day of the month; but, as the Babylonian Gemara notes upon it, that they might reduce a fortunate thing to a holy day, and an unfortunate to an unlucky day." These remarks must be borne in mind hereafter whenever we have to

---

[1] Jer. xxxi. 15.

[2] The "habit" is "general" but not invariable. There are a few exceptional cases where Matthew (*Horae Synopticae*, p. 158, referring to Mt. xxvii. 34, 43, 57) alludes to prophecy without quoting it.

[3] *Hor. Hebr.* on Mt. i. 17.

compare a rough and unsymmetrical tradition in Mark with one that is smooth and symmetrical in Matthew. Matthew will be found sometimes to have "reduced things to the very same when they were near alike."

In concluding these remarks about Matthew's arrangement of evidence, we ought to note that what may hold good about the main body of his Gospel may not hold about the last verses in which he supplies what Mark omits—some mention of the post-resurrectional appearances of Jesus to women and others. In describing the first of these it is said about the women, " They came to [him] and took hold of his feet "; and, in the second, about the eleven, " And when they saw him, they worshipped, but some doubted. And Jesus, having come to [them] spake unto them...." The prominence here given to the testimony of women is remarkable, considering that, according to Josephus and the Talmud[1], a woman's evidence was not to be received in a court of justice, and Paul makes no mention of any appearances to women.

If these narratives proceeded from the same pen that wrote the Sermon on the Mount, in apparent defiance of chronological order, we might have expected the manifestation to the disciples to come first, as being the more important, even though it was later in point of time. But there are many indications in Matthew's context that parts of it proceed from an editor, later than the compiler of the great mass of the Gospel, and freer from Jewish tendencies. The context speaks of a " saying" spread abroad "*among Jews* unto this day[2]"—the only use of the word " Jews " in Matthew, outside the phrase " King of the Jews." It contains also a precept

---

[1] Joseph. *Ant.* iv. 8. 15, *Shebuoth* 30 *a*, comp. *Acta Pilati* § 7 (A and B) "We have a law that a woman's evidence is not to be received." This exclusion of women is not sanctioned by any Biblical express statement. But the Law may assume it. The Greek and Roman custom would also probably be against the admission of such evidence.

[2] Mt. xxviii. 15.

to "baptize all nations into the name of the Father and of
the Son and of the Holy Spirit." The last words of all, " I am
with you...unto the consummation of the aeon," come much
more suitably here than this baptismal precept, which (if the
text is genuine) appears to be ante-dated.

Why does not Matthew mention the manifestation to
Peter—a character so prominent in his Gospel—which Paul,
in his list of the manifestations, places first of all? The
explanation may be as follows. The author of these Matthaean
traditions of the Resurrection is not moved by the objection
(by which Paul appears to have been influenced[1]) that "the
evidence of a woman is not to be received," so much as by
the objection that *the evidence of a single witness is not to be
received*. This objection is forcibly stated by an assailant of
the Christian religion, Celsus, in the second century. His
exact words have been preserved by Origen: "When he
[*i.e.* Jesus] was in the body and disbelieved in, he used to
preach freely to all ; but when [by continuing to do this] he
would have created a strong belief, having [as you Christians
say] risen from the dead, he [merely] appeared-by-glimpses
to *one weak-woman by herself*, and to his own mad-worshippers,
[and that,] secretly[2]."

Celsus appears to have had before him the very early
tradition preserved in the Mark-Appendix : "He appeared
*first to Mary Magdalene, from whom he had cast out seven
devils*[3]." Origen replies to him by quoting Matthew to shew
that "Mary Magdalene and the other Mary[4]" went to the
grave and that Jesus appeared, not "to one alone," but to
them, in the plural, "*that is, clearly, the above-mentioned
Marys*." Looking back to the preceding text in Matthew, we

---

[1] In 1 Cor. xv. 5—8, Paul omits all mention of manifestations to women,
but mentions three to single witnesses (1) Cephas, (2) James, (3) himself.

[2] Origen *Cels.* ii. 70 ἑνὶ μόνῳ γυναίῳ καὶ τοῖς ἑαυτοῦ θιασώταις κρύβδην
παρεφαίνετο. We have no one word in English to express γυναῖον.

[3] Mk xvi. 9.   [4] Mt. xxviii. 1.

find *two Marys and a third woman* mentioned as present at Christ's death, with others; and the Synoptic passages parallel to the passage of Matthew quoted by Origen mention *three women*[1]. Possibly, therefore, the tradition followed by Matthew was intended to mean, as the Diatessaron expresses it, blending Matthew and Luke, "Mary Magdalene and the other Mary and other women." If that could be proved, we should be able to say that, out of the three manifestations in the Mark-Appendix, the Matthaean tradition took *those which were received by more than two witnesses*[2]. In any case, Matthew seems to emphasize the necessity of *more than one*.

The last words of all—those with which Matthew's Gospel closes—concentrate the reader's thought, not—as does that Mark-Appendix—on the promise of mighty and miraculous powers of healing to be given to the disciples[3], but on the promise of Christ's perpetual presence with them in their preaching of His gospel, "till the consummation of the aeon[4]."

---

[1] Mt. xxvii. 56 (comp. Mk xv. 40), abbreviated in Mt. xxvii. 61 (comp. Mk xv. 47) and in Mt. xxviii. 1 (but three persons are mentioned in the parallel Mk xvi. 1 and comp. Lk. xxiv. 10).

[2] Comp. Deut. xvii. 6 "at the mouth of two witnesses *or three witnesses*," and see *Johannine Grammar* 2589 quoting Philo i. 243 "now a holy matter is approved through *three witnesses*." Matthew omits the manifestation to the "two," mentioned in Mk xvi. 12 (detailed in Lk. xxiv. 13 foll.).

[3] Mk xvi. 17—18.   [4] Mt. xxviii. 20.

CHAPTER X

ORDER AND ARRANGEMENT IN LUKE

§ 1. *Luke attempted to write in chronological "order"*

LUKE'S intention to write in chronological order is definitely expressed in his Preface: "Forasmuch as many have attempted[1] to draw up a narrative concerning those facts [—for facts they are, not phantasms—][2] which have been solidly-and-convincingly-fulfilled among us, even as they were delivered unto us by those who were from the beginning eyewitnesses and attendant-ministers of the Word [of the Gospel], it seemed good to me also, having followed [them] up all from the first with-exact-care, to write [them] unto thee consecutively, most excellent Theophilus, that thou mayest recognise, concerning the words [of-the-doctrine] in which thou wast schooled, [their] unshakable-truth[3]."

---

[1] "Attempted," with sense of futility or evil purpose, both in Acts ix. 29, xix. 13 (not elsewhere used in N.T.) and also in LXX, see p. 116, n. 2.

[2] Comp. Origen *Fragm. on Lk.* (Lomm. v. 86, 237) which contrasts "facts" with the φαντασία into which the Incarnation was converted by heretics.

[3] On this Preface see *Notes on N.T. Criticism* **2980—4.** Add Origen's remark on "all" ("having followed [them] up *all*") οὔ τισι τῶν εἰρημένων, ἀλλὰ πᾶσιν. Luke probably used it with reference to the preceding πραγμάτων (which signifies the words and the deeds of the real, non-phantasmal, incarnate Lord). Ἅπασι is used similarly, in the neuter, by Demosthenes, xix. § 257 " knowing his villainies most exactly *and having followed [them] all up.*"

"*Consecutively*" καθεξῆς (not in LXX or N.T. exc. Lk. and Acts) lit. "*exactly in order,*" is much rarer in literary Greek than ἐφεξῆς (not in

It will be observed that Luke applies the word "following-up[1]," not to "teaching," as the Epistles to Timothy do, but to "facts," as handed down to the believers of his day by *those who had been eyewitnesses or attendant-ministers*. This language prepares us to find, in his Gospel, traces of traditions, documentary or oral, from various apostles or disciples, and certainly from more than two. Also this "following-up with-exact-care" suggests, in this context, the existence of some degree of intricacy or obscurity in the evidence so that it was necessary to "follow up" the track, as it were, like a patient hunter, distinguishing tracks that led wrong from the track that led right.

For example, in dealing with the precepts to the Twelve, we shall find that Luke, apparently "following up the facts," came to the conclusion that Matthew, in his version of them, had combined two accounts, one by Mark, but one by another author—the former relating to the Twelve, but the latter relating to "other" Apostles, whom Luke calls "seventy." How Luke detected this we have no direct evidence to shew. But he tells us that "*the Lord*"—not "Jesus," but "*the Lord*" —sent out these "other" Apostles. Now it is very unusual for Jesus to be called "*the Lord*" in Gospel narrative. But it is easily intelligible that Luke may have had access to a collection of traditions like that which Paul has handed down concerning the Eucharist, of which Paul says "I received

LXX or N.T.) "*following in order*." The former does not occur in the Concordances to Aristotle, Epictetus, and Plutarch (except once); the latter occurs in them often. Good Attic Greek would have been content with ἑξῆς as in Lucian (*Hermotim.* § 43, i. 785) "You speak as though in every case (πάντως) letters were written *in order* (ἑξῆς), first A, secondly B...." But Luke always uses ἑξῆς (not in N.T. except Lk. vii. 11, ix. 37, Acts xxi. 1, xxv. 17, xxvii. 18) with the article, to mean "the day (*or*, time) following." For that reason, perhaps, among others, he prefers the emphatic καθεξῆς for which Steph. *Thes.* quotes one passage from Plutarch and one from Ælian.

[1] Παρακολουθέω occurs in N.T. elsewhere, only in 1 Tim. iv. 6, 2 Tim. iii. 10 and Mk-App. xvi. 17 W. H. marg.

from *the Lord* that which also I delivered unto you[1]." In such a collection, "*the Lord*" may have been regularly used for "Jesus." We shall presently come to other instances of "*the Lord*" in Luke—almost alone of the Evangelists—introducing narratives peculiar to his Gospel. These facts point to the conclusion—which is supported by other evidence —that Luke found a non-Marcan as well as a Marcan account of the Sending of Apostles, that the former was in a collection where Jesus was regularly called "the Lord," and that Luke, in the true spirit of an exact historian "following up" perplexing tracks, determined to leave the stamp of its origin on this other narrative, by retaining "*the Lord*" thus, "After these things *the Lord* appointed other seventy[2]."

We have seen, above[3], that "after these things" is an unsafe guide in chronology. Luke may have been misled here, in placing the Sending of the Seventy so soon after the Sending of the Twelve. Perhaps indeed the Sending of the Seventy—or some of its precepts, such as "eat those things that are set before you[4]"—refers to a period after the

---

[1] 1 Cor. xi. 23. In the Pauline Epistles, and in the Acts, κύριος, *with the article*, would mean "*the Lord Jesus*" (except in very special contexts such as ὁ ἄγγελος τοῦ κυρίου) in accordance with 1 Cor. viii. 6, "To us there is one God, the Father...and one Lord, *Jesus Christ*," so that Rom. xii. 11 "serving *the Lord*" (on which Origen Lat. quotes 1 Cor. viii. 6) would mean "serving *the Lord Jesus*." For the most part, "*the Lord*" and "*the Christ*" would not be used in gospels, until He had been (Rom. i. 4) "defined" by "the resurrection of the dead," to be, in a unique sense, *the* Son and Lord and Christ. The originators of the reading Lk. xxiv. 3 "the body of *the Lord Jesus*" (comp. Mk-App. xvi. 19, 20) were perhaps influenced by the feeling that Jesus had been thus "defined."

[2] Lk. x. 1.   [3] See pp. 74 foll., 80 foll.

[4] Lk. x. 8 ἐσθίετε τὰ παρατιθέμενα ὑμῖν, comp. 1 Cor. x. 27 πᾶν τὸ παρατιθέμενον ὑμῖν ἐσθίετε, *i.e.* eat, without regard to Jewish distinctions. No doubt, the context shews that Luke placed the precepts before Christ's resurrection, *e.g.* (x. 1) "The Lord sent them...into every city and place where he himself purposed to come." But might not this be used, in poetic tradition, of "the Lord sending His Apostles," *e.g.* Paul, to the

Resurrection. But at all events Luke might say "I did my best. I copied the document exactly. And I ascertained it was '*after.*' I could not ascertain "*how long* '*after.*'"

Again, take the Lucan context of the words of Jesus, "the dead are raised[1]." If they are to be taken literally, as Luke appears to take them, we require some narrative of an act of raising from the dead to justify them. Both Matthew and Luke report the words; but Luke alone inserts an account of the raising of a widow's son at Nain, from the bier on which he was being carried to the grave. This, if we overlook the plural ("are raised") as hyperbole, would justify the literal interpretation. Without this, there would be nothing in Luke to justify the literal appeal to facts. For, although Matthew has previously made mention of the raising of Jairus' daughter, Luke has not. He puts it much later[2]; and indeed, since Jesus said, in that instance, "She is not dead but sleepeth[3]," it is not a strong case. The case supplied by Luke is much stronger. Matthew, however, though he agrees with Luke as to "the dead are raised," and as to the context and circumstances in which the words were uttered, has no record of any act of revivifying except that which concerns the daughter of Jairus.

As regards the source of Luke's insertion, we should note that, here again, "*the Lord*" is used for "Jesus," not in speech but in narrative ("And when *the Lord* saw her[4]"). It is probable that Luke has inserted the story from the document above mentioned, attempting to fix its chronological place

cities of the Greeks, *e.g.* Corinth, as to which He said to Paul (Acts xviii. 10) "I have much people in this city"? On the Mission of the Seventy see *Clue* 233 foll., *From Letter to Spirit* 1015 *a* foll.

[1] Mt. xi. 5, Lk. vii. 22.   [2] Mt. ix. 23—5, Lk. viii. 52—5.
[3] This is in all the Synoptists Mk v. 39, Mt. ix. 24, Lk. viii. 52—3. They all add "they mocked him." But Luke alone adds "knowing that she had died."
[4] Lk. vii. 13. Comp. 2 Esdr. x. 1 foll. on the mother mourning for her son, *i.e.* Zion mourning for the Temple and the City.

by reference to the words of Jesus in the Double Tradition, which he has taken in a literal sense—"the dead are raised."

One more instance must suffice. The Diatessaron, giving Matthew's account of the calling of the four fishermen, who " forsook " their " nets " or " their ship " and " followed " Jesus, places immediately after it[1] a narrative of Luke describing how Jesus " saw two boats," one of which belonged to Simon, who had "toiled all night and caught nothing "; and how at His command, Simon cast the net again and caught a multitude of fishes ; and how he and his companions " left everything and followed Jesus." Possibly Luke meant to suggest that Simon, after first being called with the words " I will make you fishers of men[2]," neglected the call till he was summoned a second time in a command addressed to him alone, " Fear [thou] not, henceforth *thou* shalt be a fisher of men unto life[3]." But Luke does not say this. He gives his readers the impression that Simon had not been called before, and that the Lucan narrative is to be substituted for (not placed after) that of Mark and Matthew[4].

There are grounds for thinking that Luke may have been misled by following some Hebrew document in which the Call of Peter the Fisherman, and the Return (*i.e.* the Repentance) of Peter the Fisherman, were connected together. Luke's narrative begins with a form of words that is a sign of translation from Hebrew[5]. John has preserved some such

---

[1] Diatess. v. 48—9.   [2] Mt. iv. 19.   [3] Lk. v. 10.

[4] The narratives, as they stand in the Diatessaron, may be illustrated by the much more difficult sequence in 1 S. xvi. 22 "And Saul sent to Jesse, saying, Let David, I pray thee, stand before me ; for he hath found favour in my sight...," followed by xvii. 55—8 "And when Saul saw David go forth against the Philistine, he said unto Abner...Whose son is this youth?... Inquire thou whose son the stripling is... And Saul said to him (David), Whose son art thou, thou young man? And David answered, I am the son of thy servant Jesse..."

[5] Lk. v. 1 ἐν τῷ ἐπικεῖσθαι. On this use of ἐν τῷ see *Son of Man* 3333 *e*. In due course, as part of the examination of Lucan parallels to Mark, the

a tradition about Peter the Fisherman[1]. This he places after the Resurrection. It mentions one boat instead of two. Indeed it seems expressly to contradict one detail of Luke by saying that the net "was *not* rent[2]." Also it says that Peter swims *to* Christ instead of bidding Christ depart *from* him[3]. Nevertheless it agrees with Luke in making Peter the most prominent of the disciples in a story about a miraculous draught of fishes. This counts for a great deal in two gospels that agree so seldom.

Moreover, there are further similarities of detail. Luke first represents Jesus as "*standing by the lake Gennesaret*," and subsequently as bidding Peter let down the nets, to which Peter replies "*Master, we toiled all night and took nothing, but at thy word* I will let down the nets." John says that Peter and six other disciples went fishing, and "*in that night they took nothing*, but when day was now breaking *Jesus stood on the shore*," unrecognised ; then Jesus says "*Cast the net* on the right side of the boat, and ye shall find," and now, at last—when they have "found"—Jesus is recognised as the Lord: "That disciple whom Jesus loved saith unto Peter, 'It is the Lord,'" and Peter "threw himself into the sea," while the rest came in the boat.

In addition to these similarities it must be said that, in Luke, whereas Peter, before the miracle, calls Jesus "Master," or *Epistatés*—a word used by no Evangelist except Luke, and probably always representing "*Rabbi*"—after the miracle Peter calls Him "Lord" ("depart from me, *O Lord*"). This is not the place to discuss Luke's use of the vocative *Epistata* and its motive, and the fact that it mostly belongs to Petrine

---

facts given in **3333** *e* will be more fully illustrated, and it will be shewn that even in the Acts, where the form is comparatively rare, Hebraic influence may be traced.

[1] Jn xxi. 6—11.
[2] Lk. v. 6 διερήσσετο, Jn xxi. 11 οὐκ ἐσχίσθη.
[3] Lk. v. 8, Jn xxi. 7.

or Hebraic traditions[1]. The point for us, at this moment, is one of *thought*, not of words. The Lucan thought is, "Peter called Jesus *Master* until he was converted by the proof of a miracle. Then he called Him *Lord*." The Johannine thought is, "No miracle proved to Peter, at all events on this occasion, that he saw his Lord before him; he did not guess it till 'the disciple whom Jesus loved' said to him 'It is the Lord.' The miracle was only an instrument. Love was the agent."

It is possible that John intended, not to deny Luke's narrative, but to supplement it. But the omission of the Lucan miracle by Mark and Matthew, in the place where Luke inserts it, and the difficulty of reconciling the Lucan position with the narrative of Mark and Matthew, favour the conclusion that Luke's chronology is here in fault, and that John has preserved the truer tradition.

§ 2. *Luke wrote as a Greek historian but incorporating Jewish documents and traditions*

The only direct evidence as to Luke's purpose and plan is to be found in the Preface to the Gospel, supplemented by the Preface to the Acts. The former has been quoted above. The latter runs as follows: "The first[2] discourse

---

[1] On ἐπιστάτης (alw. voc.) see Dalman *Words*, p. 336 foll. Lk. v. 1 begins with the Hebraisms (1) ἐγένετο, (2) ἐν τῷ, on the latter of which see *Son of Man* 3333 e. There is also an ἐγένετο ἐν τῷ in the Lucan story of the ten lepers (Lk. xvii. 11—13) where ἐπιστάτα occurs. Petrine passages containing ἐπιστάτα are Lk. v. 5, viii. 45, ix. 33. John the son of Zebedee utters it in Lk. ix. 49. The other Synoptists present interesting variations, *e.g.* Mk iv. 38 διδάσκαλε, Mt. viii. 25 κύριε, parall. to Lk. viii. 24 ἐπιστάτα (where the speakers are all the disciples in the boat).

[2] "First (πρῶτον)." Why not "former (πρότερον)," as in Philo ii. 444 ὁ μὲν πρότερος λόγος ἦν ἡμῖν, ὦ Θεόδοτε, περὶ τοῦ...? Possibly because Luke does not mean, as Philo does, "former [of two]," but "first [of three, or more]." Luke may have planned a third discourse filling up the lacuna left in Acts xxviii. 30—31 "two whole years." See *Expositor*, March 1913, p. 284.

(*lit.* word) on-the-one-hand I composed about all things, O Theophilus, that Jesus began[1] both to do and to teach, up to the day when, having-given-commandment to the apostles through the Holy Spirit[2]—[those apostles] whom he [had] chosen[3]—he was taken-up [to heaven]. To whom he [had] also presented himself, living (after he [had] suffered [on the Cross]) by many proofs...[4]."

This second extract would deserve attention if only for the emphasis laid by it on the " *beginning* to do and to teach," as contrasted with the end implied in "the day" when "he was taken up." But our attention ought also to be given to another point—an apparent resemblance, here, between Luke's two Prefaces and a passage of Josephus.

The passage of Josephus occurs in a defence of the antiquity of the Jewish nation. Addressing " Epaphroditus, most excellent of men," he begins by saying that, since he sees multitudes of people accepting, as a " proof" of the recent origin of the Jews, the silence of Gentile historians concerning their antiquity, he thought it his duty to write

---

[1] "Began," *i.e.* before His death, and before the Holy Spirit was given (see below, p. 128).

[2] "Through the Holy Spirit." Perhaps Luke implies that there was some gift of the Holy Spirit when He appeared to the Apostles and (Lk. xxiv. 45 foll.) "opened their mind" and gave them their commission to preach in His name. Jn xx. 19—23 expressly describes such a gift.

[3] "Whom he had chosen." Something seems to be implied, *e.g.* "whom, *after the defection of Judas,* he had finally chosen," or, "whom, *after death,* he chose *again*" (comp. Jn vi. 70 " Did not I choose you, the twelve, and one of you is a devil ?").

[4] "*Proofs,*" τεκμηρίοις, does not recur in the whole of the canonical Greek Testament. It is a favourite word with Thucydides, who says, early in his history (i. 20—1) that though his readers may find it difficult to accept from him " *every proof [taken singly] in consecutive order* (παντὶ ἑξῆς τεκμηρίῳ)" they will nevertheless not go wrong if they accept the general results of "the above-mentioned *proofs.*" Both ἑξῆς and τεκμήριον represent the lines on which Luke writes—a history of *consecutive* facts resulting in *proofs.*

on the subject, so as to teach all that desire to know the
" truth[1]."

So far, there is no great verbal similarity. "Truth" and
"proof" are words that any writer, Jew or Gentile, was
obliged to use if he wished to begin a historical treatise with
a preface in the style of Thucydides. Also, any literary
patron might be called "most excellent." But there is much
more in the following sentences. They include some of the
words or phrases used in the Lucan Prefaces, either exactly
or nearly reproduced, such as "attempting," "delivering"
(*i.e.* handing down tradition), "with-exact-care," "following-up,"
and "eyewitnesses." They also lay the same stress on "facts"
and their "truth" :—

" Certain vile fellows have *attempted* to slander my history
...But they ought to know that whosoever promises to *hand-
down* [a history of] *actions* in-their-true-form should himself
first learn them *with-exact-care*, either *having-followed-up* the
occurrences, or inquiring about them from those that know...
Now when writing the history of the war [of the Jews with
the Romans] I had been the personal originator of many
actions, and *eyewitness* of very-many ; and, to-speak-of-the-
whole, there was nothing whatever of *the* [*things*] *said or done*
of which I was ignorant[2]."

---

[1] Joseph. *Contr. Apion.* i. 1 " *Most excellent* " is, as in Luke, κράτιστε.
But that was probably a common word in dedications, so that not much
stress must be laid on that similarity. "Proof" (or "token") is τεκμήριον.

[2] Joseph. *Contr. Apion.* i. 10. All the italicised words are identical, in
Greek, with the Lucan words above mentioned, except (1) "actions,"
πράξεις, Lk. πράγματα, and (2) "said or done" τῶν λεχθέντων ἢ πραχθέντων,
Lk. (Acts) ποιεῖν τε καὶ διδάσκειν. On (2), note that Papias (above, p. 82)
has the same phrase, but with the repeated ἤ.

That the Lucan "attempt," ἐπιχειρέω, was used by Luke in a bad
sense, is indicated by its use in LXX, in Acts, and in the present
passage of Josephus. See also Mayor's note on Clem. Alex. 889 ἐπι-
χειρήμασι, "sophisms," quoting Dion. H. p. 723 l. 10 ψυχρὰν καὶ ἀπίθανον
ἐπιχείρησιν. Versions of a fragment attributed to Origen (Cramer *ad
loc.*, and Lomm. vol. xx, pp. viii—ix) assert as (1) probable (τάχα) or

Of course, allowance must be made for the fact that all writers of history in the first century, if they wrote in Greek and in the high historical style, used Thucydides and Demosthenes as their quarries, common to all—Thucydides for phrases in narrative, and Demosthenes for phrases in intervening speeches; and it is in that style that Josephus and Luke both write in the passages we are considering[1]. Nevertheless the similarity in thought as well as in language between Josephus in addressing the " most excellent Epaphroditus," and Luke in addressing the "most excellent Theophilus" will (I believe) make it appear probable to many readers that Luke had read the treatise of Josephus against the misrepresentations of the "facts" of Jewish history, and adopted his language in his own treatise against those who (as he believed) had "attempted" to represent, in such a way as to misrepresent, the "facts" of the life of the King of the Jews[2].

Before passing from this subject we must add that Dionysius of Halicarnassus and Cicero, writing before the beginning of the Christian era, testify to the widespread imitation of Thucydides by writers of history. The general conclusion reached by Dionysius, in giving advice to writers, is that "the narrative passages are, with few exceptions, altogether admirable and adapted for every kind of service, whereas the speeches are not all suitable for imitation[3]." For speeches,

---

(2) certain ($\chi\rho\dot{\eta}$ $\nu o\epsilon\hat{\iota}\nu$) that it is used in a bad sense here. Origen might be induced by his natural moderation, and by the Aristotelian use of the word in a good sense, to suggest that there may be a doubt of the bad sense here. But the whole of his context indicates that he inclined to believe that Luke included "false prophets" in his "many."

[1] Josephus says (*Contr. Apion.* i. 9) that in writing his history he "used some assistants for the Greek ($\chi\rho\eta\sigma\acute{a}\mu\epsilon\nu os$ $\tau\iota\sigma\iota$ $\pi\rho\grave{o}s$ $\tau\grave{\eta}\nu$ $\dot{E}\lambda\lambda\eta\nu\acute{\iota}\delta a$ $\phi\omega\nu\grave{\eta}\nu$ $\sigma\nu\nu\epsilon\rho\gamma o\hat{\iota}s$)."

[2] The *Contr. Apion.* of Josephus (*Dict. Christ. Biogr.* iii. 449 a) was probably written after A.D. 93. The Preface to the Acts must therefore have been written later still, if it alludes to that treatise.

[3] *Dionysius of Halicarnassus, The Three Literary Letters*, by Professor

Dionysius preferred Demosthenes as a model for imitators. That Luke, in the Acts, imitated Thucydides in certain parts of his narrative and Demosthenes in certain of the speeches, was (in my opinion) demonstrated, by a multitude of instances, in a book printed for private circulation thirty years ago. Its author, searching the Acts for Thucydidean words or phrases rare or non-occurrent in N. T., except in Lucan writings, found no less than 82 in the 27th chapter which contains 44 verses, but only 4 in the 7th chapter which contains 60 verses. The latter contains the speech of Stephen where Thucydides would be quite out of place; the former contains Luke's account of Paul's shipwreck. The author came to the conclusion, *inter alia*, that Luke "had studied with great care the whole of the Sixth Book of Thucydides, perhaps in consequence of the visit to Syracuse," and that "he had read a large portion of the Eighth Book, probably in connexion with his voyage along the coast of Asia[1]."

W. Rhys Roberts, Litt.D. (Cambridge: at the University Press), pp. 32 and 29.

[1] *A Short Account of some Coincidences of Expression in Thucydides and the Acts of the Apostles*, by J. Hamblin Smith, M.A. (for private circulation; Cambridge, 1883), p. 68. As the book may be difficult to procure, I add a few of the similarities. On p. 2, Acts xxvii. 13—18 ἄραντες...παρελέγοντο τὴν Κρήτην...συναρπασθέντος δὲ τοῦ πλοίου... τῷ ἀνέμῳ...ἐφερόμεθα...χειμαζομένων, is compared with Thuc. vi. 104 ἄρας παρέπλει τὴν Ἰταλίαν...ἁρπασθεὶς ὑπ' ἀνέμου...ἀποφέρεται ἐς τὸ πέλαγος ...χειμασθεὶς (where note that πέλαγος is used in Acts xxvii. 5 to mean the open sea and occurs nowhere else in N.T. exc. Mt. xviii. 6 τῷ πελάγει τῆς θαλάσσης). Note also (*ib.* p. 11) the similarity of rhythm between Acts xvi. 12 εἰς Φιλίππους, ἥτις ἐστὶν πρώτη τῆς μερίδος Μακεδονίας πόλις κολωνία, and Thuc. vi. 62 ἐς Ἱμέραν, ἥπερ μόνη ἐν τούτῳ τῷ μέρει τῆς Σικελίας Ἑλλὰς πόλις ἐστί. The whole book deserves careful study. Part of it is devoted to a comparison of the language of the Acts with that in two of the most celebrated orations of Demosthenes. The conclusion seems to me to be that Luke, like most other educated Greeks, agreed with Dionysius of Halicarnassus that Thucydides and Demosthenes were good authors for him to follow when writing in the historical style with narrative and speeches intermixed.

One passage in this valuable little treatise calls attention to some Thucydidean phrases in Luke's version of the Discourse on the Last Days. In this, Mark and Matthew mention merely *limoi* "*famines*"; but Luke says "*loimoi* and *limoi*," that is, "*plagues* and *famines*." Now this recalls a well-known interchange of the two words in a prophecy mentioned by Thucydides in connection with the plague at Athens, "There shall come a Dorian war and a *famine* with it." Some said it was *famine*, some said it was *plague*. But, when the plague came, says Thucydides, men decided that *loimos*, not *limos*, had been the right version. Luke's text says that not merely *limoi*, but also *loimoi* were to come[1].

But Luke also adds "terrors and great *signs* from heaven." And, later on, he repeats "signs," saying "*signs* in the *sun and moon and stars*[2]." He also expresses the impending distress in language like that of a speech of Nicias in Thucydides and quite unlike that of the parallel Synoptists[3]. Now the speech in Thucydides is followed—not long afterwards, in point of time, though several chapters intervene—by an account of an eclipse of the moon, which so alarmed the Athenians that they delayed their purposed retreat for twenty-seven days, thereby ensuring their total discomfiture at the hands of the Syracusans[4]. It does not seem fanciful

---

[1] Mk xiii. 8, Mt. xxiv. 7, Lk. xxi. 11, see Thuc. ii. 54. The noun λοιμός occurs in Canon. LXX only in 1 K. viii. 37, Ezek. xxxvi. 29, as a various reading and error for λιμός. In the MSS of Lk. xxi. 11, the order of the two nouns varies.

[2] Lk. xxi. 25. This is parall. to a mention of the sun and moon and stars in Mk-Mt., but the preceding mention of "signs from heaven" has no Synoptic parallel.

[3] See *A Short Account* &c. pp. 55—6, which calls attention to the depressing speech of Nicias in Thuc. vi. 68, and to some similarities in the Acts, and others in the Gospel, Lk. xxi. 19— 26 στρατόπεδον = "army" (only here in N.T.), κτήσεσθε, ἀνάγκη = "distress" (Pauline), ἀπορία "desperate-condition" (only here in N.T.). All these are in one short chapter of Thucydides. There is also Lk. xxi. 26 ἀποψυχόντων "gasping" (only here in N.T.), used for "expiring," as in Thuc. i. 134.

[4] Thuc. vii. 50.

to see in these Lucan deviations from Mark and Matthew some trace of the influence of Thucydides on a writer who had himself spent "three days[1]" at Syracuse on his way to Rome with Paul.

No doubt, if Luke had been recording words of Jesus Himself, handed down with the authority of His direct utterance, he would not thus have deviated from Mark into the style of Greek history, any more than he does in recording the speech of the martyr Stephen. But this adds greatly to the importance of Luke's deviation. It indicates Luke's belief that much of the predictive part of the Discourse on the Last Days was *not* Christ's language in the ordinary sense. It was perhaps of the nature of what Eusebius calls an "oracle" given "to those of approved reputation" in Jerusalem[2].

Our conclusion is, that Luke wrote in the Greek literary style not only, as a rule, when recording what he had himself observed, but also, on rare occasions, *when he amplified a tradition inferentially for the purpose of clearness, vividness, or inclusiveness.* On other occasions he would, as far as possible, employ the language, written or oral, of those from whom he derived his information.

§ 3. *Luke's arrangement, sometimes dependent on "proofs"*

If we compare Matthew's Sermon on the Mount with Luke's parallels, we shall find the first dozen verses of the former placed (in a condensed form) at an early date by Luke.

---

[1] Acts xxviii. 12.

[2] See *Notes on N.T Criticism* **2837** (iii) *a* and *Son of Man* **3281** *a—b*. The δόκιμοι mentioned by Eusebius might be variously interpreted, *e.g.* as (Mk xiii. 3) " Peter and James and John and Andrew." Comp. Gal. ii. 6 δοκοῦντες and the context, referring to "James [*i.e.* the Lord's brother] and Cephas and John." The deviation of the parallel Matthew and Luke from Mk xiii. 3 shews that the names did not rest on the highest authority.

But the thirteenth verse (about "salt" that loses its savour) is placed by Luke some eight chapters later, after some Lucan traditions about "counting the cost" of a "tower," and "taking counsel" about a "war." Turning to Mark, we perceive that Mark, too, puts a tradition about "saltless" salt at a much later period[1]. In this case, then, we see that Luke may have depended, not merely or at all on "proofs," but on Mark's testimony in favour of postponing this utterance.

In another instance, where Matthew introduces the Lord's Prayer, as part of a continuous discourse, with "Thus therefore pray ye," the Lucan context itself seems to acknowledge doubt as to date and place: "And it came to pass in the [time of] his being *in a certain place praying*, when he ceased, a *certain one of his disciples* said unto him, 'Lord, teach us to pray, as also John taught his disciples.' And he said unto them, When ye pray, say…[2]." Here, then, we have to ask, "Was this vague introduction written by Luke himself in his own person, or copied by him as part of the traditional framework in which he received this version of the Prayer?"

This is one of the many occasions where the Hebraic construction ("in the [time of] his being") is of very great value in the attempt to analyse Luke's Gospel. For it shews us that he is not introducing the Prayer in his own Greek-history style, but that he is copying the whole—Introduction as well as Prayer—from a literal translation of some Hebrew document[3]. This document left the time and place vague, and Luke retains unaltered the phrases implying vagueness.

---

[1] Mt. v. 1—12 parall. to Lk. vi. 20—23, but Mt. v. 13 parall. to Lk. xiv. 34—5 (comp. Mk ix. 50).

[2] Lk. xi. 1 (comp. Mt. vi. 9). "In the [time of] his being" is an attempt to render ἐν τῷ εἶναι, which (see *Son of Man* 3333 *e*) is a sign of translation from Hebrew.

[3] It may be objected that Biblical Hebrew does not use the vocative "*Father*," which Luke here uses, but only "*my Father*." But in later Hebrew as well as in Aramaic, *Abba* is used to mean either "Father ' or "my Father," so that Lk. xi. 2 "Father," parall. to Mt. vi. 9 "Our

This is honest, and we ought to be grateful. But it follows that in dealing with this tradition (and others like it) Luke would be guided only by inference as to the position in which he should place it. The place he gives it is appropriate. We know from Berachoth[1] that some celebrated Rabbis gave short prayers to their several pupils to be used on occasions where brevity was needed. Missionaries would be in special need of brevity. Jesus had just appointed His missionaries, not only the Twelve, but also, according to Luke, the Seventy. Luke therefore places the Prayer after the appointment of the Seventy, and just before traditions (peculiar to his Gospel) concerning the power of "importunity" in prayer[2].

All this trouble, taken to get as near as possible to "facts" through "proofs," is worthy of a disciple of Thucydides[3]. But on the other hand Luke's desire for proofs and definite facts appears sometimes to lead him beyond the limits imposed by the older Evangelists. His preference for definite evidence may perhaps be illustrated by his difference from Matthew in the history of the birth of Jesus, where Matthew describes an unnamed angel as speaking to Joseph by night in a dream, but Luke describes the angel Gabriel as speaking to Mary in what is clearly not a dream[4]. These two traditions however, not being parallel, are not so instructive as the Synoptic parallels in the description of Christ's Baptism. There Mark and Matthew use the word "*saw*" in connection

---

Father that is in heaven" does not constitute any objection to the hypothesis that Luke is copying a literal translation of a Hebrew version of the Lord's Prayer (see Levy i. 3 *b*).

[1] *Berachoth* 29 *b* foll.　　　　[2] Lk. xi. 5—8.

[3] See Thuc. i. 20, 21 (and comp. ii. 39, 50) for references to the "proofs" from which, at an early stage of his History, he infers the facts of antiquity.

[4] Mt. i. 20 "in a dream," compared with *ib.* 24 "arose from his sleep," implies night. Lk. i. 26—8 "the angel Gabriel was sent...and, having come in unto her, said" is more definite.

with the descent of the Spirit as a dove, but Luke dispenses with "*saw*," and adds that the Spirit descended "*in a bodily shape*[1]." We have also seen how Luke appears to have been led, by a desire to find a proof of the truth of the words " the dead are raised," not only to insert in his Gospel, but also to insert just before those words, an account of a literal raising of the widow's son at Nain[2]. Even Peter, according to Luke, would seem to have been led to attach himself to Jesus, at the outset of the Gospel, not by His personality and doctrine, but by a miraculous draught of fish[3].

No doubt, the word "proofs" is never used by Luke in his Gospel and only once in the Acts; but the atmosphere of what one may call "proof-seeking" may be felt in many portions of the former where neither the word, nor any word like it, is employed. The Spirit itself is described by Luke in his Gospel as "a mouth and wisdom" which "adversaries" will not be able to "withstand or to gainsay"—a true aspect, but not the deepest or most essential[4]. And in the description of the manifestations of the Resurrection, Luke insists, as it were, on the possession of "flesh and bones" by the risen Saviour, and also on His power to "eat"; which He does, in the presence of the Eleven[5]. This indeed, from a Greek point of view, is the most cogent of the "many proofs" spoken of in the Preface to the Acts[6]. But it strangely differs from the

---

[1] Mk i. 10, Mt. iii. 16, Lk. iii. 22.
[2] See p. 111.   [3] Lk. v. 8—9.
[4] Lk. xxi. 15.
[5] Lk. xxiv. 39—43. In Jn xx. 24—9, Thomas insists on proof by touch, and it is offered to him. But he is gently rebuked, and it is not stated that he availed himself of the offer. It is said, "Because thou hast *seen* me, thou hast believed." It is not said, "Because thou hast *touched* me."
[6] Acts i. 3. In Lk. xxiv. 22—3 (speaking of "women" and "a vision of angels") it may be implied that the speakers were not at that time aware of the subsequent manifestation to the women who (Mt. xxviii. 9) clasped Christ's feet. But the intention of the context appears to be to shew that the Evangelist—like Paul, see p. 106—does not appeal for

Johannine answer to the question, " Lord, what is come to pass that thou wilt manifest thyself unto us and not unto the world?" and also from any reasonable interpretation of the words in Revelation, " If any man hear my voice and open the door, I will come in to him, and will sup with him and he with me[1]."

§ 4. *Luke's view of " the beginning" and " the end"*

The Preface to Luke's Gospel acknowledges the source of his traditions to have been "those who *from the beginning were eyewitnesses and attendant-ministers of the word*." Later on, giving us the only numerical date in his Gospel, he says " In the fifteenth year of the reign of Tiberius Caesar, Pontius Pilate being governor of Judaea...the [utterance of the] *word of God came upon John the son of Zacharias*...[2]." Is that to be regarded as the " beginning"? Ought we not rather to go back to the first words of his Gospel (as distinct from the Preface)? These are " There was *in the days of Herod, king of Judaea*, a certain priest named Zacharias." The "beginning" may be the promise of a son to Zacharias and his wife Elisabeth. Afterwards there follows the Annunciation to Mary with the words "This is *the sixth month* with her that was called barren[3]." Then the hymn of Zacharias says to the child " Thou shalt go before the face of the Lord [*i.e.* Jehovah] to make ready his ways; *to give knowledge of salvation unto his people in the remission of their sins[4]*."

These last words do not clearly define the limits of John's mission. They may be intended to mean that he was not to be himself Jehovah's *agent* in *giving* " the knowledge of

---

" proof" to women's evidence, which would not be accepted in a law-court either by Jews or by Greeks.

[1] Jn xiv. 22, Rev. iii. 20.

[2] Lk. i. 2, iii. 1—2. "Word"=λόγος, which may also mean "reason," &c. "[Utterance of the] word "=ῥῆμα.

[3] Lk. i. 5, 36.   [4] Lk. i. 76—7.

salvation" or "the remission of sins," but that he was only
to *prepare* "*the way of Jehovah*" *with a view to these gifts*
(the earthly agent, or giver, being left unmentioned). But
at all events it seems clear that Luke regards John, in a
twofold sense, as a "beginning." The promise of his birth
begins the book. Zacharias is the "eyewitness" of that
promise. John's beginning to preach is introduced with an
exactness of dating that we should expect from none but
a historian introducing a new epoch. Also we have been
invited to date the birth of Jesus Himself from that of John,
inferentially, by some words of Gabriel to Mary about "*the
sixth month* with her that was called barren[1]." This would
lead us to the conclusion that Jesus was six months younger
than John. And we are told subsequently that Jesus was
thirty years old when He "began[2]."

Out of all these *data* one might have supposed that we
could surely extract the date of Christ's birth. But we
cannot. There is a fatal defect in the facts. We are told
the exact date of John's beginning to preach, but not the
date of his birth. It is left unstated in the vagueness of the
Hebraic phrase "in the days of Herod." Also we are not
informed whether John began to preach as a youth (like
Jeremiah) or as a mature man (like Ezekiel). Luke's chronology is a mixture of solid historical facts—some of them
quite superfluous—with fatal inexactness. Who wants to
know that, as Luke tells us, "Lysanias was tetrarch of
Abilene" in "the fifteenth year of Tiberius Caesar"? What
we want to know is the interval between John's beginning to
preach and Christ's beginning to preach. And this we are
not told. It may have been ten months. It may have been
ten years.

The most reasonable supposition is that Luke himself did
not know the interval. It is hardly conceivable that, if he did

---

[1] Lk. i. 36.   [2] Lk. iii. 23.

know it, he should have failed to state it. How easy to have said about John's birth, " In the —— year of Herod the king," or " In the —— year of Augustus Caesar[1] " ! But Luke's language gives us internal evidence indicating that his original authority, and not he himself, is to blame. The first sentence of his Gospel, introducing the birth of John, closely resembles the first sentence of the book of Samuel, introducing the birth of Samuel, and has—like the greater part of the Lucan Introduction—a Hebraic and poetic sound[2]. Moreover this Introduction has no less than five instances of that Hebraic construction (the article with the infinitive) almost confined to Luke among the Evangelists, which indicates Hebraic origin in a Lucan tradition[3].

The right inference, then, from these omissions—the reasonable as well as charitable inference—is not that Luke was incapable, but that he was honest. Mixing Hebrew traditions with Greek traditions, he left the signs of the mixture. We ought to be most thankful that he did so. He might have rendered the whole into one uniform history imitative of Thucydidean Greek. Then indeed he might have deceived us. As it is, he has left us ignorant but not more ignorant than he probably was himself[4]. Luke's

---

[1] Lk. iii. 1.

[2] Comp. Lk. i. 5 " There was...a certain priest...," with 1 S. i. 1 "Now there was a certain man..." introducing Elkanah, and his wives, by name.

[3] See above, p. 112, n. 5, as to $\dot{\epsilon}\nu \tau\hat{\omega}$ with inf.; it occurs in Lk. i. 8, 21, ii. 6, 27, 43.

[4] Lk. ii. 2 (R.V.) "This was the first enrolment made when Quirinius was governor of Syria" is a pathetic attempt of Luke to supply, as far as possible, *data* for determining chronology by piling fact on fact. The sentence is not clear, and volumes have been written about it. The most reasonable supposition is that Luke took the words down just as he heard them, or read them.

The hypothesis of the incorporation of documents may best explain the similarity between Josephus *Ant.* xx. 5. 1 foll. and Acts v. 35 foll. (a speech assigned to Gamaliel addressing the Sanhedrin). The subject is *theomachy*, and the Greek word (or rather its adjective) is used in a manner that would appeal to Greeks rather than to Jews.

ignorance, however, does not alter his view—which is what we are considering. And the view he took as a historian appears to be that, according to the above-mentioned rules of *taxis* or "order," in Greek history, "nothing could well come before" the Baptist, in a treatise on the Gospel[1].

But the view taken in the Lucan Messianic genealogy appears to be inconsistent with the view taken in the whole of the Lucan Introduction, and especially in the Songs of Zacharias and Mary about the Messiah. For to whom would Simeon and Anna, and all the characters mentioned in that Introduction, have looked as the Messiah's progenitor, except to the patriarch called by Zacharias "Abraham our father[2]"? And in the hymn of Mary, the Mother of the Lord, are not the last words "Abraham and his seed for ever[3]"? Was not Matthew also content to trace the genealogy from Abraham? Why then does Luke carry it up to the first man, "the [son] of Seth, the [son] of Adam"—and then, "the [son] of God[4]"? Since every human being is a "son of Adam," must there not be some hidden meaning in these words, if they are to escape the charge of platitude?

The composite nature of Luke's Gospel makes it impossible to answer this question with any confidence. The carrying up of the genealogy to Adam may have been the result of more causes than one. First, there would certainly be the desire for a new genealogy, caused by dissatisfaction with Matthew's genealogy for reasons above mentioned[5]. Secondly, there might naturally be a feeling that this new genealogy of the Messiah should make it its main object to answer the question—natural to Greeks as well as to Jews on the introduction of a new personage to their notice—"Who, and whose son ultimately?" Thirdly, there might be a desire that the answer to the question "Whose son?" should include some allusion to the Lord's own self-appellation, "the Son of Man."

---

[1] See above, p. 83.   [2] Lk. i. 73.
[3] Lk. i. 55.   [4] Lk. iii. 38.   [5] See p. 104.

Taking this title in its Hebrew form, that is, "Son of Adam," a mystical Pauline genealogist might despise the jibe "Are we not all sons of Adam?"—by replying, "Yes, but to 'Son of Adam,' I add 'Son of God'; that means 'The Adam that is conformed to God's image.'" Moreover, there might be the influence of another Pauline doctrine, namely, that "God made *of one* every nation of men[1]," so that—all being sons of Adam, the "nations" of the Gentiles as well as "the chosen people" of Israel—it was fit that the Saviour of all should share, in some sense, the parentage of all.

Of all these possible causes one alone is certain, namely, that Luke, as being a painstaking historian, must have been dissatisfied with such a genealogy as Matthew's. The new one, which he substituted, he may have adopted as being at all events less unsatisfactory than Matthew's, copying it, just as it stood, without any intention to suggest that Adam, or Man (rather than John) was "the beginning" of the Gospel.

Turning from the "beginning" of the Gospel to Luke's conception of the "end," we find him, in the Acts, apparently dating it from the day of Ascension: "The first discourse" —he says, meaning the Gospel—deals with "all that Jesus began to do and to teach *until the day in which he was taken-up* [*to heaven*]." "Begin"—which, coming in a Preface written in literary Greek, cannot well be regarded as Hebraistically or pleonastically used—has been interpreted here in two ways, as meaning either "from beginning to end," or "began initially and rudimentarily so that the Apostles might complete the work." But in any case the day of Ascension is regarded as "the end," because nothing can be done by the Apostles in the way of preaching the gospel till they receive "power from on high[2]."

Hence the Gospel does not conclude with the completeness of a whole drama, but rather as the first of two acts in a

---

[1] Acts xvii. 26. [2] Lk. xxiv. 49.

drama. In the conclusion of Matthew, and also in the Mark-Appendix, the Apostles are sent forth with the words " Go ye[1]." In Luke the command is " Tarry ye[2]." It is true that the Gospel ends with a note of joy, " And they were continually in the temple blessing God." But there is also a subdued undertone of expectation. They are " blessing God " for a promise not yet fulfilled—a promise of " power " to conquer in a battle not yet begun.

---

[1] Mt. xxviii. 19, Mk xvi. 15.   [2] Lk. xxiv. 49.

CHAPTER XI

ORDER AND ARRANGEMENT IN JOHN

§ 1. *John arranged his narrative by the Jewish Calendar,*
interpreted spiritually

THE Jewish Calendar was most clearly distinguished from
that of the Greeks and the Romans by the continually recurring
six days of work followed by the sacred seventh day of rest.
With such a six days, implied, this Gospel begins[1]. It is the
period in which the little band of the first six[2] disciples is
created—a creation of the Church in miniature. We shall
also find that with another six days, not implied but expressed
(" *six days* before the Passover[3] ") the work of Jesus on earth
is brought to an end.

The Jewish Calendar is also distinguished by its three
great Feasts, the Passover, the Feast of Weeks, and the
Feast of Tabernacles. Of these, the first—besides its primary
purpose to commemorate the historical Deliverance from
Egypt—was connected with the agricultural year in this
respect, that, on the morrow after the sabbath in that Feast,
the sheaf of the firstfruits of the harvest was to be " waved "
before the Lord[4]. The second Feast, the Feast of Weeks—
beginning on the fiftieth day from that "waving[5]," and hence
called, in Greek, Pentecost, *i.e.* Fiftieth [Day]—celebrated

---

[1] See *Johannine Grammar* 2624, and comp. Westcott (on Jn xii. 1)
" The Gospel begins and closes with a sacred week."

[2] For "six" disciples, not mentioned but implied, see the comment in
Son of Man 3374 c on Jn i. 40—41.

[3] Jn xii. 1.   [4] Lev. xxiii. 11.   [5] Lev. xxiii. 15—16.

the conclusion of the wheat harvest, which was long after the beginning of the barley harvest. The third and last of the great Feasts, that of Tabernacles, commemorating the "tabernacling" of Israel in the desert, coincided with the time of the ingathering of fruits and the vintage. In addition to these scriptural Feasts, there was that of the Dedication of the Temple, called by the Jews "Lights," and established to commemorate the cleansing and repairing of the Temple by Judas Maccabaeus[1].

Not one of these four Feasts is mentioned by the Synoptists except the Passover. That is mentioned twice by Luke, once when Jesus went up to it as a boy of twelve, once when He went up to die on the Cross. But Mark and Matthew mention it only on the latter occasion. From the Synoptic Gospels, taken alone, we should infer, either that Christ's public life did not cover more than an exact year, or else that, if it included two or more Passovers, Jesus attended none of them but the last. John, on the other hand, mentions all the four Feasts above mentioned except the Feast of Weeks.

Unfortunately, some doubts about textual readings, and also doubts about transpositions of long passages, make it difficult to say, as to some Johannine mentions of "feasts," what Feast is meant. Still the fact remains that he expressly mentions the three that suggest spring, autumn, and winter[2],

---

[1] 1 Macc. iv. 59. See *Light on the Gospel* 3999 (iii) 7.

[2] Jn x. 22—3 "And it was the feast of dedication at Jerusalem. It *was winter*. And Jesus was walking in the temple in Solomon's porch." Why does John add "*it was winter*"? Partly, perhaps, because some readers might not know the time of this Feast, since it is not mentioned in scripture ; but partly, too, for a reason similar to that which made him write about Judas (Jn xiii. 30) "He, then, having received the sop, went out straightway : *and it was night*." The language may be, as it were, sympathetic with the subject. The Gospel has recently introduced (Jn viii. 12) the subject of the revelation of Christ as the Light of the world, and the Evangelist may wish to suggest to his readers that the Light is fast sinking towards the horizon—at least, for those unbelieving Jews who regard Him as a blasphemer.

giving them their Jewish names. Also, in describing the Feeding of the Five Thousand, John, alone of the Evangelists, speaks of the loaves as being of "barley," and he previously describes Jesus as saying to the disciples, "Say ye not, Yet four months and the harvest cometh[1]?"

The precise significance of the "barley" and the "four months" cannot be discussed here[2]; but they combine with many other expressions to shew that John regarded his Gospel as the history of a growth, a spiritual *genesis*, comprised in a revolving spiritual year. This is not a physical year of twelve solar months, but what Philo calls an "age" or *aeon*, in which there is a harrowing, and a sowing, and a watering, and a gathering in. Not that this is the one and only line of thought running right through the Gospel. There is also, as we shall see, intermixed with the thought of the annual cycle of the seed—the "grain of wheat," which, "if it die, beareth much fruit[3]"—the thought of the birth of Man, the ideal Man, Man shaped in the image of God, not without some mention of the "sorrow" that must needs be, till this "Man" is "born into the world[4]."

Further remarks on details in these aspects of Johannine arrangement must be deferred till they come before us in the regular course of our study of the Fourfold Gospel. Meantime we must note that John makes not the slightest attempt to rescue us from the chronological quagmire in

---

[1] Jn vi. 9, iv. 35.

[2] See *Son of Man* **3420**, and *Johannine Grammar* **2230** (ii) foll.

[3] Jn xii. 24.

[4] Jn xvi. 21 "The woman, *when she is bringing forth*, hath sorrow." This corresponds to Mk xiii. 8, Mt. xxiv. 8 " These things are the beginning of *travail-pangs*," which the parallel Luke omits. In Gal. iv. 19, there is perhaps a confusion of metaphor, under the influence of passionate sorrow, in which the apostle says "My little children, of whom I am again in travail until Christ be formed in you." The Socratic word μαιευτικός would not have adequately described the complex relation between the apostle and his "little children."

which Luke has left his record of Christ's life. Not a single date is given that refers to Emperor, King, Tetrarch, or Governor.

Why is this? Isaiah gives the date of his vision of Jehovah; the book of Ezekiel opens with a precise date; Luke had given a precedent for a Gospel with dates—though dates not so uniformly arranged as to be satisfactory[1]; why did not John follow Luke's precedent, but to better purpose? Was it because he would not date the coming of the Messiah by the years of a Caiaphas, or a Pilate, or any ruler of this world? Or was it because he desired to avoid, as far as possible, flagrant contradiction of the Synoptists, whom he believed to be wrong in saying—or at least in giving the impression that they meant to say—"On such and such a day John the Baptist was imprisoned by Herod Antipas, *and on that day, or a few days afterwards*, the Messiah began to preach the gospel of salvation"? The first of these questions we cannot confidently answer, though we may feel that "the fifteenth year of Tiberius Caesar" would seem strangely out of its element in Johannine atmosphere. But we can safely say that the second of these considerations—the desire to avoid open and direct contradictions of previous Evangelists —is apparent in many parts of the Fourth Gospel.

Even if John shrinks from secular dates, we might still expect that he would have given us some information about the age of Jesus when He began to preach. But the only hint on this subject is contained in the saying of the Jews " Thou art not yet fifty years old, and hast thou seen Abraham[2]?" Possibly this merely refers to the age at which Levites were relieved from laborious service. Yet so early a writer as Irenaeus not only takes it as meaning that Jesus approached the age of fifty, but also appeals, in favour of this interpretation,

---

[1] Is. vi. 1 " In the year that king Uzziah died," Ezek. i. 2 "the fifth year of king Jehoiachin's captivity," Lk. i. 5, ii. 1, iii. 1—2.

[2] Jn viii. 57 on which see *Notes on N.T. Criticism* **2989**–**90**.

to "the elders that were conversant in Asia with John the disciple of the Lord[1]." This startling statement has been (I believe) the sole early result of what Irenaeus regards as a Johannine contribution to Gospel chronology.

These facts may not suffice to shew that John did not know the exact details of the chronology of the life of Christ. But they shew at all events that he made no attempt whatever to impart such knowledge to his readers ; whereas he seems to have taken considerable pains to shew them how Christ's movements were influenced by the course of the Feasts, and how His doctrines and revelations might mystically correspond to a course, or cycle, of spiritual seasons. According to Irenaeus, those who maintained that Christ preached for no more than one year, alleged the words of Isaiah :—" to proclaim *the acceptable year* of the Lord...[2]." Luke places these words at the close of a passage of Isaiah read by Jesus in the Lord's first public appearance that he describes in detail. Having regard to other instances where John appears to substitute, for some tradition peculiar to Luke, another, externally similar but different in essence, we may fairly keep before our minds the probability that, in this case also, John had in view the Lucan chronology, and Luke's method of dating, and the inferences derived by many from "the acceptable year of the Lord" mentioned in his Gospel.

Luke's tradition—if it was his—about the literal interpretation of "the acceptable year" was one around which

[1] Iren. ii. 22. 5—6. Chrysostom (on Jn viii. 57) reads "forty" for "fifty," both in text and in comment. Early mystics, who agreed with Irenaeus, might perhaps say that the age of Jesus was about (Jn ii. 20) "forty-six years," the alleged duration of the period of building "the temple," which was "his body" (see *Johannine Grammar* 2021—4).

[2] Iren. ii. 22. 1 " They endeavour to establish this out of the prophet, for it is written (Is. lxi. 2) ' *To proclaim the acceptable year of the Lord*, and the day of retribution '—being truly blind, inasmuch as they affirm they have found out the mysteries of Bythus, yet they do not understand..." No evangelist quotes Is. lxi. 2 except Luke (iv. 19), who stops at " the Lord."

Gnostic errors were soon to cluster. Not improbably, the germs of these errors were already shooting when the Fourth Gospel was published—published perhaps, for the purpose (among other purposes) of guarding against such errors. John at all events would have agreed with what Irenaeus says about Isaiah, "The prophet speaks neither of a day that includes the space of twelve hours, nor of a year of which the length is twelve months[1]." That is the Johannine view. On the only occasions when John uses the word "year" in the singular, he speaks of Caiaphas as being "High Priest for *that year.*" But he does not mean it in the sense in which the Romans would say "consul for *that year.*" He means, as Origen repeatedly implies, High Priest *in that crisis, that period of judgment for the rulers of the Jews, when Jesus was destined to suffer death[2].*

That points, in brief, to the difference between Lucan and Johannine dating. Luke dates the coming of "the word of God" about Jesus from (*inter alia*) "Annas and Caiaphas[3]." John dates Caiaphas from Jesus.

§ 2. "*The beginning*"

About the Johannine "beginning" we shall have to speak in detail when we discuss the opening words of the Marcan Gospel, "[The] beginning of the gospel of Jesus Christ." Here we may note that John deviates from Mark and returns to the language of Genesis in his opening clause :—"*In [the] beginning....*" This prepares us for the *hexaemeron* that

---

[1] Iren. *ib.*

[2] Comp. Origen *Comm. Joann.* xxviii. 15. Ἐνιαυτός, not ἔτος, is the word here used for year. It does not occur in the Gospels except in Lk. iv. 19 (Is. lxi. 2) "the acceptable *year* of the Lord," and Jn xi. 49, 51, xviii. 13 (always about "Caiaphas, high priest for *that year*"). In Heb. ix. 7, 25, x. 1, 3, it refers to the official acts of the High Priest "once in the year" or "year by year."

[3] Lk. iii. 2 "...in the highpriesthood of Annas and Caiaphas, the word of God came...."

follows. This also avoids some metaphysical speculations that might have arisen out of a personification of the Arché, or Beginning, if he had written, "*The beginning* was." In the next place, by saying "In [the] beginning was the *Logos,* or *Word,*" he calls up thoughts both of the creative Word ("by *the Word of the Lord* were the heavens made"), and also of the prophetic Word, which every reader of the LXX would find at the beginning of the books of the prophets ("*the Word of the Lord* that came unto Hosea[1]"). In Greek, too, Word, when expressed by Logos, etymologically implies orderly arrangement of thoughts, sometimes expressed in words, but sometimes not.

Thus John satisfies the canon of Dionysius[2] by giving us "a beginning before which nothing could well come." And if we reply "No, for God must come before everything, even before the Logos," he answers, "But there never was a time when God 'came before the Logos.' There never was a time when it could not be said, 'The Logos was with God.' For *the Logos was in the beginning with God.*"

After this, in two or three short sentences, John stimulates us to free ourselves from slavery to conventional metaphor by giving us two metaphors, both true. In the creative Word, he says, "there was life." Every living thing owed its life to the Logos. Yes, but in men the debt was deeper than in other living things: "The life was *the light of men.*" Was it not also "the light" of animals? Have not animals eyes? The Evangelist would of course reply "You know I mean the light of reason and the spirit." We are therefore to think of the Logos sometimes as spiritual life, sometimes as spiritual light, while not forgetting that through the Logos there were also made the material types of these spiritual things.

That is one of the steps by which the Prologue leads us

---

[1] In the LXX the minor prophets come first, and Hosea first of all.
[2] See above, p. 83.

up to a point of view whence we can contemplate the preparation for the Incarnation of the Word. The next step is
to put on one side as insoluble the problem of God's permission
of evil. While always regarding evil as evil, we are to regard
it also as, in some mysterious way, subserving good, and the
evil as a foil to the good. John does not say this. But he
suggests it to us, as it were, through Nature, by reminding us
that the darkness is a foil to the light: " The light shineth in
the darkness, and the darkness overcame it not."

Why " *the* darkness"? We can understand " *the* " in " *the*
light," for light has been mentioned before. But what is the
meaning of " *the* darkness," since "darkness" has not been
mentioned before? The first Biblical instance of "darkness"
and the first of "light" are without the article—" *Darkness*
was upon the face of the deep" and "Let there be *light*."
Not till afterwards is it said that "God saw *the light*...and
God divided *the light* from *the darkness*." But in the very
first instance in the Johannine prologue it appears to be
assumed that "darkness" is one of *the* recognised elements
(like " *the* air," " *the* sea," " *the* earth"). The first Genesis
speaks of it for the first time as "darkness" (not " *the* darkness") and as existing, not as created. In the second Genesis
it is perhaps to be regarded as " *the* darkness" because of the
aeons during which it has been striving to "overcome," and
has not "overcome," the light that "shines in it."

But whence, and why, *any* "darkness"? Does not the
Johannine Epistle imply that it would have been more like
"God" to have given us "light" and "no darkness at all[1]"?
John brings us face to face with this question and then leaves
us to answer it, so far as it can be answered at present, through
his gospel of the Incarnation. In this, he says, in effect: " It
is true that the mind of man cannot conceive that an Almighty
Goodness should permit evil. But I do not call on you to

---

[1] Comp. 1 Jn i. 5 " *God* is *light*, and in him is *no darkness at all*."

conceive at present of God as Almighty, but rather as Light contending against Darkness, and as the Father sending His Son, surely not without a divine sacrifice on the Father's part, to die for 'the light' in order that it may not be 'overcome' by 'the darkness.' Put aside therefore anxious questionings about 'the darkness.' It will be found, when it has been utterly 'overcome,' that 'the light has been shining in it'."

§ 3. *The Johannine Genealogy*

After these brief and pregnant utterances of a positive nature about what was "in the beginning," the Evangelist proceeds to negations. In these, he is apparently alluding to the three Synoptic traditions about "the beginning." Mark might be interpreted as saying "John the Baptist was the beginning"; Matthew's Genealogy as saying "Abraham was the beginning"; Luke's Genealogy as saying "Adam the son of God was the beginning."

Supplementing, or correcting, these three interpretations, the Fourth Gospel says, in effect, "John was not the Light but a mere witness to the Light. He was also a mere 'human being.' He merely '*came into existence.*' The Logos eternally '*was.*' No mere human being—and therefore neither John, nor Abraham, nor Adam—could have been 'the beginning of the gospel.' But the Logos was the Light that is continually coming into the world and illuminating every human being. And in this Gospel the Logos will soon be heard declaring, 'Before Abraham came into existence I AM.'"

"As to the genealogy of the incarnate Logos"—so the Prologue seems to say—"there is no need to trace it here according to the flesh in particular detail. Enough to say here that He 'became flesh'—that is, became flesh, not from this or that parentage, nor for this or that nation, but for all helpless flesh and blood in every nation and in all time. All were His own, but His own received Him not into their hearts. Yet to those that received Him, that is, those who believed in His name, He gave authority to become children of God, 'begotten from God.'"

Human beings to become "begotten from God"! We are naturally led on to ask "What Being, save God Himself, could bestow on humanity this divine 'authority'? Surely this Bestower, this Logos, must have been Himself essentially and uniquely *God-begotten.*" Having led us to frame this question, and to answer it for ourselves in the term "God-begotten," the Evangelist now, as it were, sanctions our answer by his description of the beginning of Genesis on earth corresponding to the beginning of the Genesis in heaven :— "The Word became flesh, and tabernacled in [the midst of] us—and we beheld his glory, glory as of *the only begotten from the Father*—full of grace and truth."

If this view of the Johannine Prologue is justified we may say that the Evangelist writes it in a twofold spirit, revealing new truth and correcting new distortions of old truth. As the author of a separate Gospel, in which he records his own vision of the glory of the Only Begotten, he frames the beginning of his work, as a poet frames the beginning of his poem, so that it may accord with its sequel and with its close. But, as being the writer of a Gospel that is in some sense not separate, but the latest of many, and as one knowing the difficulties and sympathizing with the distractions that arose in the Church from a multitude of gospel-writers, he does not reject all reference or allusion to the doctrines taught by the most authoritative of his predecessors, where such reference or allusion rose naturally to his mind in the attempt to express his own thought with brevity and force in a consistent and harmonious completeness.

Take, for example, John's introduction of the term "the Only Begotten from the Father" following the statement that "as many as received" the Logos "were begotten...from

God[1]." If anyone were to say that John wrote this simply
to meet objections arising out of the Genealogies of Matthew
and of Luke, where Matthew mentions "begotten" and Luke
does not, he would justly be condemned as a pedant. But
let us put the matter in a fairer and fuller way before our
minds, trying to realise the anxious discussions in the Church
about the two Genealogies, and the attacks brought against
them by unbelievers. Against Luke, for example, an argument, not altogether without force, though relying mainly
on our sense of the ridiculous, might be brought as follows :

"Matthew in his genealogy has a perpetually recurring
'begat'; beginning with 'Abraham *begat* Isaac' and ending
with 'Jacob *begat* Joseph, the husband of Mary....' Luke
dexterously avoids inconvenient questions about '*begetting*,'
by using the form 'son of' and turning the genealogy upside
down so as to begin 'the son (as was supposed) of Joseph,
the [son] of Heli &c.' But of course Luke must admit that
'the [son] of' means 'begotten by.' That being the case,
it is fair to substitute 'begotten by' as we ascend in the
genealogy. And now mark the result at the summit :—
'begotten by Seth, begotten by Adam, *begotten by God*.'
Adam is supposed to be, not created by God, but *begotten
by God*! This is new doctrine indeed."

If such attacks were made—and it is hardly possible that
they should not have been made at an early date—it is no dis-
paragement to John that he should have borne them in mind,
perhaps for many years, while developing his simple and
spiritual view of the essential genealogy that connected God
and Man. Seeing the truth in this immaterial aspect John
says, in effect, "Luke's text, though bald and liable to mis-
construction, contains a truth. God *did* purpose from the
beginning to 'beget' Man. 'Beget,' not 'create,' *does* express
God's purpose about Man. The creation of the first Adam,

---

[1] Jn i. 13 (R.V. marg.). The sense is spoiled, in this particular context,
by substituting " were born " for " were begotten."

after the flesh, was but the type of the begetting of the second Adam, after the Spirit. It is a paradox, but a truth, that the Logos is 'the Only Begotten,' and yet that men also, so far as they receive the Logos, are 'begotten from God.'"

§ 4. *The Johannine sequence of events*

It is perhaps in the introduction of the doctrine of the forgiveness of sins that the Synoptic sequence of events seems most abrupt. There is nothing that explains, and very little that suggests, by what stages Jesus prepared His disciples, and much less the outside world, for that critical moment when He said to the paralysed man, " Thy sins are forgiven thee." It is true that, in Mark, " belief " has been previously mentioned in Christ's first precept, "Repent ye and *believe in the gospel."* But this, coming at the outset of the Gospel, might lead some readers to protest, "We are only just beginning to read what you have written, beginning with the words '*the gospel* of Jesus Christ'; and you tell us that the first precept of Jesus Christ was ' Repent and believe in *the gospel.'* How could they, his hearers, believe in it till they had heard it ? And how can we, your readers, believe in it till we have read it ? " Perhaps Matthew and Luke felt this difficulty. At all events Matthew omits the difficult words, and Luke substitutes something quite different[1].

The Fourth Gospel, in its Prologue, goes at once to the root of the difficulty by shewing this " belief " to be not really "belief in *the words contained in a Gospel,*" but belief in the incarnate Word, belief in God's incarnate " only begotten " Son, "full of grace and truth." " As many as *received him* "— these and only these could be helped by Him. They " received " Him by " believing " in His "name[2]," that is, by

---

[1] Mk i. 15 parall. to Mt. iv. 17 "Repent ye, for the kingdom of heaven is at hand." Luke iv. 14—15 gives no precept of any kind.

[2] Jn i. 12.

accepting Him in their heart of hearts as the supreme Word representing the supreme Mind, the Son representing the Father. Receiving this leavening belief into their hearts they found their inmost nature transformed by the Spirit of Sonship.

After the Prologue comes the testimony of John the Baptist, culminating in the words " Behold the Lamb of God." These words are twice repeated. And now the herald prophet, having delivered this twofold attestation, retires into the background while the Son comes forward, and the history of the Church begins. It opens with the introduction of the first two of those faithful ones, those lovers of righteousness and truth, through whom it was destined that the world should realise that " the life was the light of men "—the first to " receive " by " believing." These prospective disciples are described as " following " Jesus. To them He utters His first words as recorded in this Gospel. And whereas Mark makes them a warning and a command[1], " The season is fulfilled...Repent ye...," John makes them a question, " What seek ye ? " Greeks would say that this way of beginning to teach was more Socratic ; psychologists, that it was more attractive and educative ; Philo and the Jews, that it had a precedent in the first Biblical utterance of " What seekest thou ? " proceeding from Conscience, or from the Angel Gabriel[2].

To this question the future converts—one of them Andrew, introduced as " Andrew, Simon Peter's brother[3] "—reply with

---

[1] In Mk i. 14—15 "preaching the gospel of God (?) and saying ([καὶ λέγων]) *that* (ὅτι) the season is fulfilled and the kingdom of God hath drawn near. Repent and believe...," the text is doubtful ; but in any case ὅτι probably means "that" (not "because").

[2] See *Son of Man* **3380** quoting Gen. xxxvii. 15 "What seekest thou?" with the comments of Philo and the Targum, who severally describe the question as proceeding from (1) the Man, *Elenchus, i.e.* the Convictor or Reprover, or (2) Gabriel, comp. Jn xvi. 8.

[3] This suggests the first thought, "Andrew, known best as the brother

another question, "Rabbi, where abidest thou?" and receive the promise "Come, and ye shall see." That, in itself, is a teacher's triumph, to induce the learner to ask questions. And the nature of the question should be noted. They do not say "Master, what shall we do to inherit eternal life?" or "What shall we do to be saved[1]?" They are drawn toward Jesus as steel to the magnet. A Jew might also say that, if turning to God's prophet means turning to God, then these two converts are, in the Jewish sense, "repenting." For repentance is denoted, always in thought, and often in language, by such "turning" or "returning."

But, for the purpose of illustrating the present context, the attraction of the magnet is a more suitable metaphor, because the two converts are themselves magnetized and receive a portion of their Master's magnetic power to draw souls. Both of the converts—it is not said that either is converted, but conversion is assumed—draw their brothers severally to Jesus[2]. How much is here left to the imagination! Of all that Jesus said during this momentous sowing of the seed nothing is recorded except "What seek ye?", "Come, and ye shall see," and "Thou art Simon, son of John, thou shalt be called Cephas[3]."

The author of the Fourth Gospel habitually represents Jesus, and all the numerous characters that he introduces to us, as speaking in one style, and that the Evangelist's own, quite different from the language attributed to Jesus by the three Synoptists in passages where they all agree. We cannot therefore be sure that any of these brief sayings are exactly historical. The writer may have been influenced by

---

of the much more famous Simon Peter," and then the second thought, "Yes, but after all, he was before Peter in coming to Jesus, and he brought Peter to Jesus. We should not have guessed this from Mark, Matthew, and Luke."

[1] Comp. Mk x. 17, Acts ii. 37, xvi. 30.
[2] See *Son of Man* 3626 a.   [3] Jn i. 42.

a desire to neutralise a tendency to magnify the position of Simon Peter as "*first*" of the Twelve[1]. And a desire to magnify Christ's insight and foreknowledge, and to shew that He "knew what was in man[2]," may have also led him to antedate the saying about Peter's name.

Nevertheless many will feel that on spiritual lines this narrative leads us to the essence of historical truth. Historically, we may say that it is more likely that Peter was converted by Christ's personal influence than by a miraculous draught of fishes narrated by Luke, and by no other Evangelist. Many things recorded by Mark in a cold abridgment were probably, in their original shape, dramatic and often repeated utterances, susceptible of variations of meaning in various circumstances and contexts. And spiritually, this vivid description of converts drawing converts to the source whence they themselves had received life, after "abiding with" Jesus, gives us (I think) a view of Jesus more in accordance with fact than that which describes Him as calling the fishermen, without any such preparation, and with a mere "follow me."

§ 5. *The Forgiveness of Sins*

Now, with the view of illustrating, by contrast, the Johannine method, let us touch on the first Synoptic account of a forgiveness of sins. When Jesus says to the paralysed man, "Thy sins are forgiven thee," if we ask, "Why did Jesus select this man as the first to be forgiven?" the Synoptists all reply, in effect, "He *saw their faith*[3]." No doubt, this is

---

[1] Mt. x. 2 "*First*, Simon...." "First" is omitted in the parall. Mk iii. 16, Lk. vi. 14. Jn i. 41 "He (*i.e.* Andrew) findeth *first...Simon*," suggests that "Simon" might have been originally connected with "first," without any notion of primacy. And it expressly asserts that Andrew, rather than Peter, was "*first*" in priority of calling.

[2] Jn ii. 25.

[3] Mk ii. 5, Mt. ix. 2, Lk v. 20. On this see *Son of Man* 3158—68. The abruptness and *anacoluthon* of the words in Mk ii. 10 and parall.—which

a true explanation, if "*faith*" is rightly interpreted. But of what kind was this "*faith*"? Was it a faith in Jesus as being merely a man of such a nature—or maybe a prophet of such a nature—that He could heal "anyone whom He liked" to heal, if only one could induce Him to "like" to do it? If it had been nothing more than this, and if this paralysed sufferer had been a rich rascal, who had paid four other men—all sharing the same "faith," a very strong faith, of its kind—to get the start, so to speak, of the other wretched sufferers that could not force their way through the door, by taking off the roof and letting him down through the opening, can we suppose for a moment that Jesus would have said to him "Thy rascalities are forgiven thee"?

No, we may be quite sure that the faith, both of this paralysed man and of his bearers, was of a higher kind than this. We do not know the special circumstances of the case; but John leads us to the conclusion that in every such case special circumstances must have existed, and that Jesus, on this occasion, whether He knew them or not, knew the man's heart, and knew that here was a case for His healing intervention. Luke has taught us the same lesson in his story—peculiar to his Gospel—of Christ's forgiving the sins of a woman who "was a sinner." The reason there given is not mere repentance, though there was repentance, but—"she loved much[1]."

These facts help to explain why John never uses the noun "*faith*"—a chameleon word that takes its colour from its atmosphere. Yet he lays stress all the more on "*having-faith*," or "*believing*," provided that one believes in the right way and in the right object—fixing one's eyes on the Suffering

---

have caused some to doubt their historical character—appear to me life-like and reminiscent of fact. And the disagreements of the Synoptists as to *circumstance* enhance the force of their evidence as to *that about which they all agree*, namely, that Jesus did pronounce a forgiveness of sins.

[1] Lk. vii. 47.

Physician, the Living Antidote of Sin, so strangely typified by the Brazen Serpent in the Wilderness ; on " Him whom they pierced" on the Cross ; on the sacrificed Son, as one with the sacrificing Father[1]. Among John's views of forgiveness, one is that it is a "giving forth," from the Father through the Son, of spiritual health to the spiritually diseased ; and it is also sometimes suggested that the Son, while He " gives forth " this divine righteousness, also takes away the human sin— taking it as it were on Himself, as Jesus took on Himself the defilements of His disciples on His last night with them, when He " began to wash the disciples' feet and to wipe them with the towel wherewith he was girded," thus signifying how He " loved them to the end[2]."

§ 6. *Attraction and recoil, Peter and Judas*

It is this doctrine of Messianic forgiving by Messianic self-imparting, that, according to John, alienated many of Christ's disciples as well as the multitude. The alienation follows the Feeding of the Five Thousand and indeed is a consequence of it, though not the first consequence. The first consequence was a quite opposite one : " They said, This is of a truth the prophet that cometh into the world " ; and they " were about to come and take him by force, to make him king[3]." But when Jesus developed His doctrine He found Himself deserted by so many of His disciples that He said to the Twelve " Can it be that ye too desire to go away?" Then followed Peter's confession, " Lord, to whom shall we

---

[1] This thought of the Son as being "delivered over," or " given," by the Father, to suffer for men, is lost in our rendering of the Synoptic passages where the English uses "*betrayed*," that is, "betrayed *by Judas*." The Greek is "*delivered over*." That may mean "delivered over *by God*," *i.e.* to die for mankind. See pp. 151—2, and *Paradosis* 1150 foll. and *passim*.

[2] Jn xiii. 1 foll. On the "wiping," and its spiritual significance, see Origen *ad loc.* (Lomm. ii. 401).

[3] Jn vi. 14—15.

go ? Thou hast words of eternal life. And we have believed and know that thou art the Holy One of God[1]."

The corresponding confession of Peter in the Synoptists is placed by Luke immediately after the Feeding of the Five Thousand[2], and by Mark and Matthew not long after the Feeding of the Four Thousand[3]. In all the Gospels, the circumstances appear to show that the confession took place in a crisis, when Jesus was unpopular and almost deserted. But the Synoptists give us no hint as to the cause of the unpopularity. The Fourth Gospel gives more than a hint. It records first the murmuring of "the Jews," and then that of "his disciples." They themselves say about His doctrine, "This is a hard saying; who can hear it[4]?" This is historically probable, and it throws light upon the Institution of the Lord's Supper. John omits the Institution—probably as being recorded by all three Synoptists, and as being acted on in all Christian Churches with such a degree of uniformity that it was not well to introduce a fourth tradition—but he alone inserts the doctrine that seems to have prepared the way for it.

The Johannine form also of Peter's confession should be noted as pointing to the secret of Christ's influence and to the recognition of that secret in the Fourth Gospel. The confession in the Synoptists is, at its fullest, "Thou art the Christ, the Son of the living God[5]." But in John it is less conventional :—"We entirely believe and entirely know that thou art the Holy One of God[6]." And this is preceded by

---

[1] Jn vi. 68.   [2] Lk. ix. 17—18 foll.

[3] Mk viii. 9, 27—9, Mt. xv. 39, xvi. 13—16.

[4] Jn vi. 41, 60.

[5] Mt. xvi. 16. Lk. ix. 20 omits "the Son" and "living," Mk viii. 29 omits "the Son...God."

[6] Jn vi. 69 πεπιστεύκαμεν καὶ ἐγνώκαμεν. The R.V. "we *have* believed" would naturally mean "we *have* believed up to this time, or, at times, but we do not now believe." The Greek perfect here denotes completeness.

"Lord, to whom shall we go? Thou hast words of eternal life." These preceding words indicate the source of the confession. The Spirit of Jesus had already to some extent passed into Simon the son of John, preparing to convert him into Cephas, or Peter, a rock of faith. Jesus had already so far made Himself King in the apostle's heart as to make Himself necessary, deposing[1], so to speak, even for the future, all other powers that might claim to rule there.

The more one reflects on these facts, the more improbable will it appear (I think) that at this crisis, or near this crisis, Jesus should have said to Peter "Go behind me, Satan," as Mark and Matthew say. It will be shewn, in its order, that the narratives of Mark and Matthew shew possibilities of misunderstanding. They point to an original that mentioned "Peter" and "Satan" but not as they understood it. And it is hardly possible to exaggerate the importance of the fact that *the parallel Luke—agreeing closely, for the rest, with Mark and Matthew—omits the rebuke to Peter*[2]. It would be most discreditable to Luke's knowledge, if he was ignorant of this tradition; or to his honesty, if he knew of it, and knew it to be true, and yet suppressed it. But it is not discreditable to him if he omitted it, knowing that there was *some* misunderstanding, but not knowing exactly what the misunderstanding was.

This is a clear case for Johannine intervention. And it will be shewn, I think, that there are good grounds for believing that John not only intervenes, but also indicates what he considers to be the truth at the bottom of the error. There were actually sayings of Jesus at this time, about "*going*" and "*behind*" (or "*back*") and "*Satan*" (or "*devil*"). Also,

---

[1] Comp. *Richard II*, v. i. 28 "Hath Bolingbroke depos'd thine intellect? hath he been in thy heart?"

[2] Lk. ix. 22—3 closely follows Mk viii. 31, 34, Mt. xvi. 21, 24, but has no parallel to Mk viii. 32—3 and Mt. xvi. 22—3, which contain the rebuke of Peter as "Satan."

one of these sayings was addressed to *"Simon Peter."* But *the " devil" was not " Simon Peter" but "Judas the son of Simon Iscariot*[1]*."*

Antecedently there is much to be said for this interpretation. It is easily credible that a disciple of worldly ambition, who followed Jesus for what he hoped to get, saw his hopes collapse, one by one, when, in the first place, Jesus withdrew from the multitude that would have made Him king, and then rebuked them for seeking " loaves and fishes," and finally explained away His Messianic promises into what seems even now to some modern Christians, and with much more reason must have seemed to Christ's disciples then, " a hard saying[2]." When many of His disciples *"went back,"* and when the Lord said to the Twelve " Do ye also desire to *go* ?" Judas did not indeed *"go"* at that time ; but he was at work among the Twelve—so John appears to suggest—as the Adversary or Satan, urging them to constrain the Master, for the Master's good, to become " king "; and Jesus detected his attempts to lead the Twelve in this direction. It was for this reason that, in reply to Simon Peter's confession " Thou art the Holy One of God," He said, " Was it not I that chose [all of] you, the Twelve, and one of you is a devil[3]? "

Reading between the lines of what follows, and reading in the light of the Mark-Matthew tradition, we ought to be able to keep our minds open to a demonstration that the Evangelist is really explaining that there was no reference at all to *Simon Peter.* It was *Judas the son of Simon*: " *But he was speaking of Judas [the son] of Simon-Iscariot*; for he [*i.e.* Judas, not Simon] was destined to deliver him up, being [also] one of the Twelve."

---

[1] Jn vi. 71. John, alone of the Evangelists, says (thrice) that Judas (Iscariot) was "son of Simon." "The son of Simon," meaning "Judas," might in some circumstances—particularly in Greek, "son" being omitted —be confused with "Simon."

[2] Jn vi. 60.   [3] Jn vi. 70.

If Jesus said to Peter, as the faithful representative of the Twelve, in contrast with Judas the incipient traitor, "*Goest thou behind Satan?*" that is, "Wouldst thou too follow Judas?" the alteration of a single letter would convert the pathetic but obscure question into a bitter, but perfectly clear, rebuke "*Go back, Satan!*" Such a rebuke Mark has recorded, and Matthew has followed him, though faintly attempting to dull the sharp point of the rebuke by adding an explanation, "Thou art my stumbling-block." But Luke's omission, and John's explanation, should go far to convince us that there is some misunderstanding, and that Peter, with all his faults, never received the name of "Satan" from the lips of his Master[1].

§ 7. *John's omission of exorcisms and of most of the predictions about "betrayal"*

No one can reasonably doubt that Mark, followed by Luke, is right in declaring that Jesus came at first before the multitudes in the character of an exorcizing as well as healing Prophet, one to whom the devils cried out "We know thee who thou art, the Holy One of God[2]." John's omission of Christ's acts of exorcism can be explained from a feeling that they were but superficial manifestations of His power and that enough had been said about them. He tells us himself that when Jesus was in Jerusalem at the first Passover, "many believed on his name, beholding his signs" —presumably acts of healing—and that Nicodemus inferred

---

[1] On this passage, and on the Biblical use of ὀπίσω, and ὑπάγειν, and corresponding Hebrew words, see *Son of Man* **3528** *b*, *From Letter to Spirit* **891** *b*. It should have been added in the former that "*Go, Satan*" is inserted by Matthew, but omitted by Luke, in that one of the three temptations (relating to "*the kingdoms of the earth*") which is most closely connected with the Johannine tradition that the multitude sought to "snatch" Jesus away "that they might make him a *king*."

[2] Comp. Mk i. 24, Lk. iv. 34.

from them that He was "a teacher come from God." But he adds that Jesus did not "trust himself" to those who thus "believed," and that He rebuked Nicodemus for what was, in effect, incapacity to grasp the nature of the conditions for entering into the kingdom of God[1].

Yet these and other Johannine disparagements of belief based on "signs" must not lead us to suppose that John regards Mark as historically wrong. John himself says that Jesus, before the first visit to the Passover, "went down *to Capernaum*...and abode there not many days[2]." Now the Synoptists all say, or assume, that Capernaum was the principal scene of Christ's "mighty works." We may therefore suppose that the first outburst of popular amazement at Christ's "mighty works at Capernaum" took place during that early visit, and that John, so to speak, clears away these rudimentary manifestations of power, in a brief mention of a brief stay in that city, before he brings Jesus up to Jerusalem. It is not in Capernaum but in Jerusalem, and in the Temple, that the great battle begins. According to Mark and Luke, the battle began in a synagogue, between Jesus the Exorcist and a demoniac, or the devils that possessed him[3]. But according to John, it began in the Temple. And Jesus, the representative of the true Temple, is seen contending against the ruler of this world; who sets up his throne in the House of the Lord, among them that "sold oxen and sheep and doves," making the Father's House "a house of merchandise."

As regards the predictions of " betrayal," or (more correctly) of "being delivered over," it is much more probable that Jesus

---

[1] Jn ii. 23 foll.

[2] Jn ii. 12. Comp. Lk. iv. 23 " Whatsoever we have heard done at Capernaum." Luke has not yet mentioned any mighty works as " done at Capernaum." But he assumes that they had been done, and were well known in Nazareth.

[3] Mk i. 23 foll., Lk. iv. 33 foll. Matthew omits this, though closely agreeing (vii. 29) with Mk i. 22.

associated them with the prophecy of Hosea about "the third day" than with any expectation of being "betrayed" by Judas. Hosea prophesied concerning the spiritual Israel that although "smitten" it would be restored to life: "On the third day he will raise us up and we shall live in his sight." This prophecy, in a form that identifies Jesus Himself with the spiritual Israel, the Temple of the Lord, John places in the forefront of Christ's preaching of the gospel: "Destroy this temple and in three days I will raise it up." This will have to be considered with other Johannine passages in which to be "lifted up," or "glorified," appears to be used where the Synoptists would have said "killed" or "crucified." Allowance must be made for Johannine optimism as well as for Synoptic literalism. When the comparison is finished, our conclusion will be (I think) that, although the Synoptists are closer to the letter of Christ's words, they have sometimes misunderstood it, while John, though departing entirely from the letter, does not seem to have misunderstood the spirit.

As regards some other important matters, the Johannine Targum—if we may so call it—seems closer to Christ's meaning than is anything that we can find in the Synoptists. For example, though they all mention a baptism with the Holy Spirit, they do not explain what it is. They say that Jesus taught His disciples to become as little children in some way or ways; but the way or ways they do not clearly define. And they nowhere connect this doctrine with baptism. John does connect the two. He says that Jesus—or rather, as he is careful to add, not Jesus but His disciples—continued the Baptist's practice of baptizing with water. But he introduces one of the leading Jewish teachers, Nicodemus, in a dialogue with Jesus by night, in which it is implied that the true baptism is a process of being "*born from above.*" Reading this in the light of the Prologue ("*begotten from God,*" "*Only Begotten*") we are led to infer that each disciple of Christ is to take into himself a sonship like that of Christ.

Lastly, the Synoptists describe Jesus as unexpectedly and abruptly giving Himself to His disciples at the Last Supper. John declares that He was doing this in some sense from the first, and that it was a fundamental doctrine with Him that, as the Father gives Himself to and for the Son, so does the Son give Himself to, and for, the brethren.

§ 8. *The "self-troubling" of Jesus*

In hazarding the remark that it is "more natural" to suppose this or that about Christ's teaching, as, for example, about the Eucharistic doctrine mentioned at the end of the last section, one has to meet the objection that, about a Person of two natures, human and divine, it is a contradiction in terms to say "That He should do this is *more natural* than that He should do that."

"The Johannine Christ," some may say, "is not, and cannot be, 'natural' in any ordinary sense of the word." And, in support of their view, they may allege the passage in which Jesus is said to have "troubled himself" at the grave of Lazarus[1]. Indirectly, this self-troubling of Jesus bears on the question of Johannine arrangement, so that it may receive consideration here.

I am unable to deny that there is some truth in this charge of Johannine non-naturalness. To me the author of the Fourth Gospel seems here to be attempting the impossible. In describing Christ as "troubling himself," he is trying to express something that neither he nor anyone else can express ; and he fails. But it is still possible that we ought to praise the failure as being no less helpful, in its way, than Mark's

---

[1] Jn xi. 33 (see R.V. marg.). Ἐτάραξεν ἑαυτόν, in Greek, could mean nothing but "troubled himself." When John means "was troubled," he writes (xiii. 21) ἐταράχθη. Westcott (on Jn xi. 33) quotes the Vulg. "turbavit se ipsum" and Augustine's comment "turbatus est Christus quia voluit," see *Johannine Grammar* **2614** *c*.

absolute success in describing Christ's exorcism wrought for
the child of the father who cried, " I believe, help thou mine
unbelief."

From one point of view, this doctrine of " self-troubling "
may be in part explained as a Johannine intervention to
prevent a misunderstanding of some words of Jesus in Mark
and Matthew, omitted by Luke, " Exceeding sorrowful is my
soul, unto death[1]." These words might give the impression
that Jesus was troubled on His own account, and not for
the disciples, not for the world, not for the Darkness striving
to overcome the Light[2]. They might also give rise to
discussions of an unprofitable kind about the " soul " of Jesus[3].
Perhaps it is for this reason that Luke omits them[4].

Apart from arguments derived from Luke's omission
of these words, it is easy to see that they might be used
against the Christian faith. This would be all the more
likely toward the end of the first century because of the
prevalence of the Stoic doctrine of *the duty of preserving*
"*freedom from trouble*," popularised by Epictetus. The
substance of the Manual of Epictetus was circulated, we may
be sure, long before Arrian published his notes of his master's
lectures ; and it would find readers just in those classes where
Christianity might look for some of its best converts. The
Manual tells us that when we " see anyone weeping for the
death of a child," we are not to be hurried away by our
sympathy into the vain thought that the sufferer is really
" *in evil*," for (according to Epictetus) nothing external is
really evil to anyone; it is only the man's fancying it to
be evil that makes it evil to him:—" Nevertheless, as far as
concerns [sympathetic] talk, do not hesitate to make yourself

---

[1] Mk xiv. 34, Mt. xxvi. 38.
[2] See Jerome on Mt. xxvi. 38.
[3] See Origen *Cels.* ii. 9. In *De Princip.* II. viii. 4, IV. i. 31, Origen
quotes Mt. xxvi. 38 along with Jn xii. 27 " Now is my *soul* troubled."
[4] See *From Letter to Spirit* **919** foll.

his partner ; yes, and maybe even to share a sigh [outwardly] with him. *Yet take good care not to sigh within*[1]."

What John, in effect, replies to Epictetus—indirectly through several passages of his Gospel, but especially and most directly through the story of the Raising of Lazarus— appears to be something of this kind, " Our Master *when He 'saw' those whom He loved 'weeping' for the death of one whom they, and He too, had ' loved*[2],' did not disdain to be ' *troubled* ' along with them. He, too, ' *wept*.' He did not confine Himself to sympathetic ' *talk*.' He ' *troubled Himself*.' That is, He welcomed trouble and gave it harbourage in His heart, so that it was veritably ' *in Himself*.' *In Himself* He felt a sympathy with the sufferers, and not in a mere external expression, not in a superficial self that was not His real self[3]. And by reason of this ' *self-troubling*,' He wrought His greatest work of healing, restoring to life one who had been four days dead. Thus the ' *love* ' and the ' *tears* ' and the ' *trouble*,' of the Messiah's friends and of the Messiah Himself, combined to fulfil His promise to the dead man's sister, that she should ' see the glory of God.' "

§ 9. *The Raising of Lazarus, one of three stages of "glory"*

At this point it becomes necessary to say a few words at once about a subject of which a fuller consideration must be reserved till we reach the fourfold tradition of the Riding into Jerusalem. The Johannine account of that triumphant Entry makes the Raising of Lazarus the central cause, as

---

[1] Epict. *Ench.* xvi. Comp. *Ench.* i. where the promise is made, in effect, "You will never *be troubled*," and *ib.* iii. "when he [*i.e.* your child] dies you will not *be troubled*."

[2] The "love" of Jesus for Lazarus or his sisters is mentioned in Jn xi. 3, 5, 36.

[3] Jn xi. 33, on which see *Son of Man* **3547**, or *Johannine Vocabulary* **1713** *e*, **1811** *a—c*.

it were, of the triumph, thus: "The multitude therefore *that was with him when he called Lazarus out of the tomb and raised him from the dead, bare witness. For this cause also the multitude went and met him, for that they had heard that he had done this sign*[1]." It was said above that John very seldom plainly and openly contradicts the Synoptists; but this insertion closely approaches a contradiction. For it is almost as if he said to his predecessors: "You describe the crowd as welcoming Jesus with cries of 'Hosanna' or 'king[2].' And so they did. But you do not tell your readers *for what cause* they did it. There is no sequence in your story. It was a procession of the Prince of Life. You paint the procession and a Prince, but not the Prince of Life."

Whatever may be the ultimate result of research into that most difficult of Gospel problems, the story of the Raising of Lazarus, three conclusions must be admitted by all: 1st, the omission of the act, if the act is historical, by the Synoptists, implies an astounding ignorance, or an astounding suppression of fact (a suppression that has never yet been explained except by hypotheses of a far-fetched and almost absurd nature); 2nd, John's pathetic narrative of it, taken by itself, makes it extremely difficult—and, when combined with the above-quoted "*for this cause*," makes it almost impossible—to believe that he recorded it as a mere parable or poem about Jesus as the Saviour of helpless humanity bound in the bands of sin[3]; 3rd, it is almost incredible that such a

---

[1] Jn xii. 17—18.

[2] Mk xi. 10, Mt. xxi. 9 have "Hosanna," Lk. xix. 38 has "King," Jn xii. 13 has both.

[3] It is of course quite true that picturesque details are often the mark of a late form of a tradition of which the early form did not contain such details. See *From Letter to Spirit* **1069** (i) foll., and *Notes on N.T. Criticism* **2837** foll., **2949—51** and Preface. One of the most pathetic and poetic descriptions in Hebrew poetry may be found in the Targumistic detailed account of Abraham's binding of Isaac on Mount Moriah. But the Targumist does not invent anything that is fundamental. When he

researcher as Luke, who (alone of the Synoptists) mentions Martha and her sister Mary, should have been ignorant of the fact—if it was a fact—that their brother was called Lazarus and had been raised from the dead after lying four days in the grave.

In an article on Lazarus in the Encyclopaedia Biblica, published in 1902, I endeavoured to shew how John's narrative might have been based in part on misunderstandings arising out of Luke. But that article did not take into account the following considerations, which, in my judgment, should some-what modify the conclusion, there arrived at, that the Raising of Lazarus is a "poem." True, it was explained that "poem" did not mean "invention." But that explanation did not go far enough. I should now like to submit to the reader four facts omitted in that article.

(1) The Riding of Jesus into Jerusalem was really the termination of a long triumphal procession of disciples, acclaiming Jesus as the Son of David. It began from Jericho, where He had healed one or two blind men who had appealed to Him by that title. Other passages in the Gospels indicate that this was the title by which Jesus was popularly hailed as the Healer of those dominated by Satan and especially of those afflicted with blindness[1].

(2) During the whole of this procession Mark mentions the healing of only one blind man. But the parallel Matthew

appears to do so, as in the story of Abraham's being cast into a "furnace" by Nimrod, it will often be found that the apparent invention is simply a new interpretation of the old Scripture (e.g. "*Ur* of the Chaldees" inter-preted as "*furnace* of the Chaldees," s. *Son of Man* **3369** *b*, **3501** *f* foll.). The Targumist often illustrates, and sometimes vivifies and illuminates by his amplifications ; but, as a rule, he does not invent. The same statement applies (I believe) to much Johannine matter that is regarded by some modern critics as "mere poetry," often meaning "mere fiction."

[1] One of the most remarkable is peculiar to Matthew, who says that when Jesus healed a man "possessed with a devil, blind and dumb," all the multitudes (xii. 23) "were amazed and said, Is this the son of David?"

mentions two[1]; and it is antecedently probable that in a crowd of pilgrims and disciples, raised to a high pitch of excitement by one or two acts of faith-healing near the gates of Jericho, many more such acts would follow before the procession had passed into the gates of the Temple in Jerusalem.

(3) Accordingly Luke says that as Jesus "was now drawing nigh, [even] at the descent of the mount of Olives, the whole multitude of the disciples began to rejoice and praise God with a loud voice for all the mighty works which they were seeing (*or*, had been seeing)[2]."

(4) Matthew expressly says that, as soon as Jesus had purified the Temple, "the blind and the lame came to him in the temple and he healed them[3]."

(5) Mark mentions no act of faith-healing except the one near Jericho. Nor is there any direct or clear reference to such acts on the part of the crowd. If there is any such allusion it is perhaps to be found in the words "Blessed is the kingdom that cometh, [the kingdom] of our father David," which may refer to the recent triumph of Jesus, as Son of David, over the powers of darkness in the healing of Bartimaeus. Those who shouted in the crowd might understand this, and indeed might assume it as a matter of course. But very few readers of Mark would understand it.

(6) According to the Rule of Johannine Intervention, we should expect John—if he believed Jesus to have worked

---

[1] Mt. xx. 30. Mt. ix. 27 "two blind men...thou son of David" is a separate narrative, peculiar to Matthew, but noticeable as containing the appeal to the "son of David."

[2] Lk. xix. 37 εἶδον would naturally refer to miracles going on, if not before their eyes, at all events during the course of the procession, so as to include the healing of the blind near Jericho.

[3] Mt. xxi. 14. See Origen (on 2 S. v. 6—8) "though they [*i.e.* the blind and the lame on the walls of Jerusalem] hated David's soul, yet they obtained compassion." But I have not found any links connecting Mt. xxi. 14 with 2 S. v. 6 in early Christian thought.

such a sign as the Raising of Lazarus—to introduce a mention of it at this stage and to explain thereby both the excitement of the people, and also what they meant by their shouts of " David." John would say, in effect, " 'The kingdom of our father David ' was the multitude's way of expressing God's Covenant of Life, as set forth by Isaiah, saying, 'Come unto me ; hear and *your soul shall live* ; and I will make an ever-lasting covenant with you, even *the sure mercies of David*[1].' The multitude believed that God had made this covenant with Jesus, as the Prince of Life, because they had seen all His signs. And of all these signs the greatest was that which He had worked on Lazarus, whom He raised from the dead."

In any case, no study of the order and arrangement of the Fourth Gospel can be otherwise than misleading, unless it frankly recognises that John, whether right or wrong historically, regards the Raising of Lazarus as one of three definite stages of glory through pain, by which the Son is to return on His path of ascension to the bosom of the Father. The first mention of " glory" (after the Prologue) occurs in the sign at Cana, the feast of the new wine of the gospel of life and light. This is accompanied by no suggestion of trouble or conflict—though even here there is a hint of divergence that may prepare the way for trouble ("woman, what have I to do with thee?"), and the contrast between "the good wine" and that which is "worse" seems to prepare the way for a resistance of the "worse" to the "good[2]." But from the moment when Jesus said, " Destroy this temple," there begins the process of the destruction of the old, and the preparation for the erection of the new. This conflict is at its height when Lazarus is

---

[1] Is. lv. 3, quoted in Acts xiii. 34 "And as concerning that he raised him from the dead...he hath spoken on this wise, I will give you *the holy and sure* [*blessings*] *of David.*"

[2] Jn ii. 11 "Jesus...manifested his glory," and see Jn ii. 4, 10.

raised by the Messiah—"weeping[1]" and "rebuking[2] in the spirit." In that moment a triumph is achieved over Death, and the sisters of Lazarus "see the glory of God." That is the first stage of "trouble" with its accompanying "glory."

The second stage is when the "Greeks"—who may be called "the wise men from the west" corresponding, in their attitude, to "the wise men from the east" in Matthew, and yet how different!—come forward to "see Jesus," while in the background the Pharisees, with thoughts of murder, are murmuring to one another "Behold how ye prevail nothing: lo, the world is gone after him[3]." Jesus recognises that the time has come "that the Son of Man should be *glorified*" and that "the grain of wheat" should "die" that it may "bear much fruit." For the second time "trouble" falls upon Him. "Now hath my soul been troubled." But He refuses to say to the Father "Save me from this hour[4]." He cries, "Father, glorify thy name," and receives the answer "I have both glorified it and will glorify it again." Upon this Jesus exclaims "Now is there judgment of this world. Now shall the ruler of this world be cast out." This is the second stage of "trouble"— trouble because of the hostility of the rulers of His own people, who have given themselves over to "the ruler of this world," trouble at the prospect of death at the hands of His countrymen; but "glory" and victory and "fruit" in the coming of "the Greeks" and in the advent of "judgment." Thus a second time "glory" comes hand in hand with

---

[1] Jn xi. 35 (δακρύω). Luke also (xix. 41 κλαίω) represents Jesus as "weeping." But He achieves no victory by it. It is a weeping over an irrevocable past, over sins that have already resulted in an unalterable present darkness, behind which lies imminent destruction (Lk. xix. 42) "If thou hadst known...but now *they are hid from thine eyes.*"

[2] See *Son of Man* **3547**, and *Johannine Vocabulary* **1811** *a—c.*

[3] Jn xii. 20 "Now there were certain Greeks..." is immediately preceded by the words of the Pharisees "Behold how ye prevail nothing...", meaning, in effect, "Nothing but death can stop it."

[4] Jn xii. 27, on which see *Johannine Grammar* **2512** *b.*

"·trouble," and, perhaps, a deeper trouble than before—not self-trouble now, but "trouble" of the "soul" from a cause that the Saviour feels to be outside Himself.

The third and last stage of trouble and glory is reached when Jesus is "*troubled in the spirit*[1]." "One of you," He says to His disciples, "will betray me." To the disciple whom He loves He reveals the future traitor by a sign, giving the bread dipped in wine to Judas. Are we to suppose that this was a last attempt of Jesus—acting against His own knowledge of the fruitlessness of the attempt—to reclaim Judas and to prove Himself a false prophet? Or was it done merely for the sake of the Eleven that they might not say afterwards, with shaken faith, "Our Master was good, but too good, too trustful; He did not know what it would have been well that He should know: He could not discern the false metal from the true"? Or was it done from mingled motives by the Son, looking to the Father, and leaving the matter in His hands?

That we shall never know—nor even know, for certain, what the Evangelist intended us precisely to infer. But he certainly testifies that once more, for the third and last time, trouble went hand in hand with glory: "When, therefore, he was gone out, Jesus saith, Now is the Son of Man *glorified*, and God is glorified in him. And God shall *glorify* him in himself, and straightway shall he *glorify* him[2]."

As compared with the Mark-Matthew tradition, "My soul is exceeding sorrowful, even unto death," this Johannine saying may seem superior in its exalted rapture. But is it not almost too superior, too exalted, too calm, and too cold? Coming at the moment when Judas, the lost soul, has "gone out straightway," is not this threefold emphasis on "being glorified" a little out of place? "And it was night," adds the Evangelist. "Night" indeed! Is it a time to think of "being glorified"?

---

[1] Jn xiii. 21.   [2] Jn xiii. 31—2.

No, it is not a time to think of "being glorified" in the ordinary sense of the term. But what if "being glorified" means here what a man of the world would call "being crucified"? Do we feel disposed to complain that Jesus does not weep over Judas as He wept at the grave of Lazarus? If we do, is it not because we have failed to realise that Jesus has done more for Judas than mere weeping? He has been "troubled *in the spirit.*" Not now in the "*soul,*" but in the "*spirit.*" Are we not intended by the Evangelist to perceive herein the deepest of all the "troubles" of Jesus? And does he not also wish us to try to imagine, however faintly, how profound and piercing must have been that stab of sin which penetrated that infinite calm of the Lord's inmost being through the treachery of His "familiar friend"?

Perhaps also, in reply to our remonstrance as to the incongruity of "glory" here, the Evangelist might say "Satan had just pierced the Lord Jesus with the cruellest of his arrows, and was it fit that He should weep as one incurably wounded or utterly defeated? Could He do more for Judas than be crucified for him, as also for the whole of the world of sinners lying under Satan's rule? Was it not right that in thus accepting the Cross, in this bitterest of trials, as coming to Him from the Father, through Satan, and through Judas who had made himself Satan's servant, He should bless God for this supreme 'glory' in which sin was made subservient to salvation?"

Whatever may be our conclusion as to the degree of John's spiritual or moral success in this instance, we ought not to reject the evidence of the three instances, taken together, of concomitant "trouble" and "glory." These indicate a definite Johannine intention, namely, to shew that the kind of "trouble" felt by Jesus, and handed down by Him to be felt by His disciples, was a better, a nobler, and a more blessed possession than that untroubled calm which a cold philosophy might impart to some, if they could carry out the Epictetian precept of never "sharing a sigh" with those whom they loved, except on condition of *not* "*sighing within.*"

§ 10. *The "end" and the "postscript"*

"The end," in a biography of a great man, a doer of great deeds, may be regarded in two senses. It may denote the appropriate and artistic termination of the writer's book, the book being regarded as a work of art; or it may denote the record of the last days of the man's life. If the life contains the elements of a drama, it will end with something done. What is done may be glorious victory; or it may be disastrous defeat; or it may be, as is the case with most men, a mixture of much defeat with a little victory. But in any case a dramatic biography of a great man, a man of action as well as utterance, not a mere man of letters or man of words—is commonly expected to end in some visible and splendid result. It may be the building of an empire, or it may be the conflagration of an empire. Either will seem an appropriate end. But that a biography should as it were fizzle out in vapour or smoke, with a correction of some misunderstanding or misreport of one particular saying of the great man to one particular friend, or with a complaint on the part of the biographer that he has attempted a task too large for his pen—this, we should mostly say, is inappropriate.

Judging the Fourth Gospel by this standard, we should most of us feel constrained to say at first sight, that, whether regarded as a drama or as a chronological biography, it has no appropriate "end." Yet we must also admit that this absence of end, so far from being inartistic, is almost too artistic. It risks the charge of artificiality in its apparent artlessness.

But, before going further, we must observe that the book has two terminations, first, what we should like to call "the real end," and secondly, what we should like to call "the postscript." The real end comes at the end of the last chapter but one, as follows : " Many other signs therefore did Jesus in the presence of the disciples, which have not been written in this book; but these have been written that ye may believe that Jesus is the Christ, the Son of God, and that, believing, ye may have life in his name[1]." This, though not vividly dramatic, at all events states the object of the book as a whole, and gives it a kind of unity by carrying our thoughts back to the " *life* " and the " *believing* " and the " *Only begotten* " in the Prologue.

There, speaking in his own person, the Evangelist tells the world that whatsoever was in the Logos "was *life*"; and that "the *life* was the light of men "; and that " John came to bear witness about the light that all men might *believe* through it[2]"; because the light, coming into the world, and lighting every man, came at last in such a way that "the Logos became flesh, and tabernacled among us, and we beheld his glory, glory as of the *Only begotten* from the Father." So now, turning to his readers and addressing them in the second person before he leaves them, he speaks about the " signs " wrought by the incarnate Logos, and more especially about those wrought by Him " in the presence of the disciples," and, apparently, after His resurrection. Concerning these he says, in effect, " There were many others of the same kind. But I have written these alone, in full, that ye may *believe* in Him, as being the *Life* of men, 'not overcome' by Death, and as being the Light of men, 'not overcome' by Darkness. And thus, receiving the *Only begotten* of the Father, you will receive that *life* which exists in the divine *Sonship*."

If this had been the end of the Gospel, though it would not have been so picturesque an end as either Matthew's

---

[1] Jn xx. 30—31.   [2] See *Johannine Grammar* 2303—4.

or Luke's, it would have been appropriate to the tone of the whole work and correspondent with its beginning.

Why, then, is the Evangelist not contented with this? Why does he go on to add a postscript as if to say: " In speaking of the ' many other signs that Jesus did in the presence of the disciples,' I ought perhaps to have mentioned one, in which He gave bread and fish to seven of them, by the shore of the sea of Tiberias. *This [being] now [added, makes] the third [manifestation in which] Jesus was manifested to the disciples having been raised from the dead[1]* "?

Before trying to answer this question we ought to ascertain what precisely is meant by " *the third.*" Does he mean "the third in the whole number of the actual appearances"? If so, how are we to reconcile it with " He appeared to Cephas ; then to the twelve ; then he appeared to above five hundred brethren at once...then he appeared to James ; then to all the apostles,...and last of all...he appeared unto me[2] "?

Probably John means " *third in the list of the appearances to disciples collectively,* not to disciples singly and not to the women." For this exclusive distinction he prepared us in the preceding clause, "many other signs...*in the presence of the disciples,*" and now he repeats it in " the third [manifestation in which] *Jesus was manifested to the disciples.*" Looking at the appearances to " *the disciples* " as arranged in the Diatessaron, we find, first, a blending of Luke and John, including —according to Luke, but not according to John—the statement that Jesus "ate before them[3]." Secondly comes a Johannine

---

[1] Jn xxi. 1—14. [2] 1 Cor. xv. 5—8.

[3] Diatess. liv. 1 foll., combining Lk. xxiv. 36 foll. with Jn xx. 19 foll. It will be found that the Diatessaron, in spite of its skill, does not quite succeed in combining Luke and John. For it begins by saying that (Lk. xxiv. 33) "*the eleven*" were "gathered" and that Jesus "came and stood among them," and yet goes on to say (Jn xx. 24) "But Thomas, one of the twelve...was not there with the disciples when Jesus came." Strictly speaking, the Harmonist should have said " *the eleven with the exception of Thomas*" ; but he prefers to retain the Lucan "*eleven,*" and to shew, by

(but not Lucan) account of a manifestation to the disciples including Thomas. Thirdly—and we must note that it is third—in the Diatessaron, comes this Johannine account of a manifestation at the Sea of Tiberias to seven disciples. In this, He is not said to "eat." But He causes to eat, giving food—"bread" and "fish"—to the disciples. Coming thus *third* in the Diatessaron the manifestation is perceived to be one that might naturally be called "third" by John.

It will be observed that in the second manifestation John does not deny that Jesus "ate." He merely refrains from inserting it, and passes on to say, "There was a third manifestation in which Jesus is not said to have eaten, but is said to have caused the disciples to eat." There is a great difference here between Luke and John, in spirit, though no contradictions in letter. In Luke, the "eating" is one of those external "many proofs[1]" on which he lays stress; but in John the invitation of the Lord to "breakfast" is of the nature of a mystery, a spiritual *viaticum* preparing the disciples to go forth on the way of the Cross. They feed, not on "five loaves," and these of "barley," but on the one loaf and the one fish, *i.e.* the One Body[2]. The "disciples" include Nathanael, so that they are not confined to those who are ordinarily known as the members of the Twelve. In fact, they are probably identical with the six that were called at the beginning of the Gospel, before the feast of Cana, with the addition of Thomas the Doubter.

§ 11. *The personal nature of the "postscript"*

Is there any other reason, beside this initial call, for the selection of these six? Let us look at the list. Peter, the Denier, comes first; Thomas, the Doubter, second; Nathanael

---

what follows, that "*the eleven*" is loosely used for "*a meeting of the Apostles.*"

[1] Acts i. 3. [2] See *Son of Man* **3422** *i*.

—who began by decrying a Messiah that could come from Nazareth—comes third. In these, we may see a reason. Also, if we adopt the general belief that "two other of his disciples[1]" means Andrew and Philip, we can perhaps find a reason for their presence, too. In the rudimentary mystery of the Feeding of the Five Thousand on the loaves of barley, Philip said "Two hundred pennyworth would not suffice," and Andrew said of the five loaves "What are these among so many?"—utterances that might be described as, in some sense, those of "doubters." From a poetic or mystical point of view, there would be a kind of fitness in their being selected to take part in a higher mystery that shall bring them to a closer knowledge of the true Bread.

But there remain "the sons of Zebedee." What are they recorded to have done (in any of the Four Gospels) that would secure for them a place in this little band of imperfect souls—friends all the more dear to Jesus perhaps because of their imperfections, and perhaps to be regarded as all selected for this privileged meal in order to have their imperfections cleansed away? If we can find anything of such a kind recorded by Mark, but omitted by Luke, John (according to the rule so far ascertained) is bound to intervene, and here, perhaps, is a place where we might look for such an intervention.

According to Mark, "the sons of Zebedee" came to Jesus, saying, "Grant that we may sit, one on thy right hand and one on thy left hand in thy glory," where Matthew says that the request was made by their mother, and Luke omits the whole[2]. Jesus replies, according to Mark, that, although the two brothers shall drink the cup that He will drink, and be

---

[1] Jn xxi. 2. Comp. *Evang. Petr.* § 14 "But I, Simon Peter, and Andrew my brother, having taken our nets, departed to the sea, and there was with us Levi the son of Alpheus, whom the Lord...." Here the MS breaks off. Some might identify this "Levi" (*Son of Man* 3375 *k*) with Nathanael. *Evang. Petr.* appears to be on the point of describing a manifestation of the risen Saviour parallel to the one in Jn xxi. 1 foll.

[2] Mk x. 35, Mt. xx. 20, Lk. om.

baptized with the baptism with which He will be baptized, yet to sit by the side of the throne is only "for those for whom it is prepared." Matthew also has this, but with the omission of the words about "baptism." Luke omits, of course, the reply as well as the question.

An obvious reason for Luke's omission is this, that the words appear to refer to martyrdom, and that, according to ancient tradition, John the son of Zebedee did not die as a martyr. Here, then, appears a case where the Johannine Gospel, if it intervenes, might naturally try to shew that John the son of Zebedee, martyr or not, was not below the level of the martyrs. That the subject was discussed in writing long before Jerome's days appears from his comment on the passage of Matthew : " If we read *the ecclesiastical histories* in which it is said that he too [*i.e.* John], as well as James, was cast, for the sake of martyrdom, into a vessel of boiling oil, and came-forth[1] thence as an athlete to receive the crown of Christ, and was straightway relegated to the isle of Patmos, we shall see that his mind fell not short of martyrdom, and that he drank the cup of confession—as also did the Three Youths in the fiery furnace, although the persecutor did not shed their blood[2]." Some distinction was perhaps drawn

---

[1] " Came-forth." Comp. Clem. Alex. p. 595 (quoting Heracleon) οὐ γὰρ πάντες οἱ σωζόμενοι ὡμολόγησαν...καὶ ἐξῆλθον. Ἐξῆλθον, in such cases, would generally mean " departed from life." But it might sometimes mean " *went forth* to receive execution of the sentence pronounced from the tribunal." Heracleon says that Matthew, Philip, Thomas, and Levi, belonged to this negative list. Jerome asserts, in effect, that John did *not* belong to this list. It is a pity that Jerome does not quote, or enable us to identify, the "ecclesiastical histories." The history of Eusebius does not mention the "burning oil." But Tertullian *De Prae-script. Haer.* 36 mentions it, while connecting Peter, Paul, and John, as the three pre-eminent martyrs in Rome. See *Notes on N.T. Criticism* **2939**.

[2] Origen (Lomm. iv. 15, 18) on Mt. xx. 22 says that most people refer both the "cup" and the "baptism" to martyrdom without distinguishing the shades of meaning, and he quotes Rev. i. 9 to shew that John, as well

between "baptism" and "cup," when applied to martyrs. "Baptism" implied baptism in one's own blood, poured forth for Christ in death ; "cup" might imply anguish, but not death. These facts perhaps explain why Matthew omitted "baptism" since it did not technically apply to John. They may also explain why Luke (not being quite sure about the exact words or their exact meaning) omitted the whole.

Now in the Manifestation to the Seven there is a perfectly clear allusion to the martyrdom of Peter and a fairly clear allusion to what we may call the non-martyrdom of John. After predicting Peter's death[1], the Lord says to him "Follow me," that is, as the context shews, "Follow me on the way to martyrdom on the Cross." Peter obeys the command. But, "turning round," he sees the beloved disciple also "following," although the latter had received no command. Then Peter puts the question, "But Lord, what of him?" He receives the answer, "If I will that he abide till I come, what is that to thee ? Follow thou me." It is added, " There went forth therefore among the brethren this saying, ' That disciple is not to die.' Yet Jesus said not unto him[2] 'He is

---

as James, was a martyr, Διδάσκει δὲ τὰ περὶ τοῦ μαρτυρίου ἑαυτοῦ Ἰωάννης... φάσκων (Rev. i. 9) "Ἐγὼ Ἰωάννης...διὰ τὸν λόγον τοῦ θεοῦ," καὶ τὰ ἑξῆς, just stopping short of the words καὶ (διὰ) τὴν μαρτυρίαν Ἰησοῦ. This passage, and that from Jerome, should be added to those collected in *Notes on N.T. Criticism* 2935—41, on "The Modern Hypothesis of the Early Death of John the son of Zebedee."

[1] Jn xxi. 18—19.

[2] Jn xxi. 23 "Unto him," *i.e.* unto Peter. But why is "unto him" added? Is it intended to emphasize the fact that the words were part of *a revelation to Peter, and to him alone*, and imparted by him to the beloved disciple ? D has "There went-forth this saying to the brethren and they supposed (ἔδοξαν) that that disciple was not to die (οὐκ ἀποθνήσκει) ; and [yet] Jesus said not precisely-that (αὐτὸ) (*d*, illud) 'Thou art not to die (οὐκ ἀποθνήσκεις),' but...." SS is rendered by Prof. Burkitt "But Jesus—not for that he was not to die said he [it], but...." Codex *a*, Chrysostom, and Nonnus, omit "*unto him.*" Codex *e* has "Thou shalt not die."

not to die,' but 'If I will &c....' This is the disciple that beareth-witness of these things...and we know that his witness is true."

§ 12 *Peter "following" and the Beloved Disciple "tarrying"*

We shall not understand the full force of this contrast between Peter and John unless we remember that the same Greek word means both "martyr" and "bearer-of-witness." Jesus says, in effect, to Peter, "Follow me to the Cross and be my *witness* (or *martyr*) there," and, concerning John, "It may be he shall abide till I come and be my *witness* (or, *martyr*) here," meaning "Whether following, or abiding, both are my *martyrs*." Origen, quoting the words of John about Patmos, " I, John, your brother and partaker with you in the tribulation and kingdom and hopeful-endurance in Jesus, was in the island called Patmos *for the sake of the word of God*," stops short there (with "and so on"), omitting the following words "and for the sake of *the bearing-witness* [*marturiā*] *of Christ*." But he adds that in these words John "informs us about his own *bearing-witness* (*marturion*), not saying *who condemned him*." This clause—"not saying who condemned him"—clearly assumes that the *marturiā* here implied *marturion*, and that the deportation to Patmos was the punishment of one who was, in effect, a "martyr[1]."

We have therefore to put ourselves (as the author of the Fourth Gospel does) in the position of John the son of Zebedee, regarded as a would-be and indeed an actual "martyr" in the strict sense of the term, but not (so to speak) a "blood-martyr." He is a drinker of the "cup," but not a partaker of the "baptism" of his Master. We have also

---

[1] Steph. *Thes.* mentions, as a meaning of μαρτύριον, "place of martyrdom," but not "*death-by-martyrdom*." But Lightfoot on Clem. Rom. *Cor.* § 5 quotes Euseb. *Mart. Pal.* § 11 πρὸ τοῦ μαρτυρίου διὰ καυτήρων ὑπομονῆς τὸν τῆς ὁμολογίας διαθλήσας ἀγῶνα, and Origen (*Comm. Matth.* xvi. 6) uses it thus several times.

to remember that this same John had been one of three to whom it had been said, in effect (according to Matthew), "Ye shall not taste death till ye see me come in my kingdom"; but Mark spoke of the "coming" of "the kingdom of God"; Luke omitted "coming[1]."

What did it all mean? And what did it mean for John in particular? Was it all fulfilled for him when he and James, with Peter, went up with the Master to the Mount of Transfiguration? On that day, not only Peter but also he and his brother James, had been privileged to hear the Voice from the overshadowing cloud. The Voice from heaven would naturally be connected with the thought of thunder; and he and his brother had been specially called by their Master, Boanerges, that is, "Sons of Thunder[2]." Not, of course, that they were to thunder, as if aping God, with mimic thunder of human contrivance[3]. Rather, as Origen says, they were to send forth to men the utterances of the divine thunder, being indeed, not thunders, but Sons of Thunder, "begotten from the mightyvoicedness of God, who thunders and shouts mightily from heaven to those who have ears and are wise[4]." Since that day, his brother James had "tasted death," the first of the apostles to bear witness as a martyr. Then Peter had done the same. Why had not he, too, the lingering survivor of the three, been allowed to

---

[1] Mk ix. 1, Mt. xvi. 28, Lk. ix. 27.

[2] On "thunder" and "voice" see *From Letter to Spirit* 727—9 &c.

[3] Comp. Virgil *Aeneid* vi. 585 foll., on the thunders of Salmoneus.

[4] Origen *Comm. Matth.* xii. 32. On "Boanerges" see *Son of Man* 3468 *a—b*, and note that Mark (iii. 17) John (xii. 29) and Revelation (iv. 5, vi. 1 &c.) are the only N.T. books that mention "thunder." In Jn xii. 29, "the multitude" gives the name of "thunder" to that which John records as an articulate "voice from heaven." Rev. x. 4 "*seal up* the utterances of the seven thunders" must not be taken to represent the *general* characteristic of "the sons of thunder." Their *general* task would be as Origen says, not to "seal up," but to "have ears, and be wise," and to transmit the heaven-sent revelation, as far as possible, to others.

bear witness in the same way, the blessed and honourable way of the Cross, and to " taste death " for his Master?

To this question the Evangelist, writing in the name of the beloved disciple, offers no reply derived directly from that disciple. But, as we have seen above, a mysterious answer came indirectly through Peter—after the latter had received the command "follow me," and had "turned round," or "returned[1]," and had seen "the disciple whom Jesus loved, following." The Lord had said to Peter concerning that disciple " *If* I will that he abide till I come, what is that to thee?" There was an " *if.*" Nothing was certain. Yet the saying had " gone forth to the brethren," in a definite form, that he was "not to die " till the Lord's coming. The disciple wished to deprecate this. Such a saying—like some sayings in the Epistles and the Acts, might lead the brethren to restless expectations of the Lord's immediate "coming" in catastrophic fashion, with fires of wrath and armies of avenging angels, judging and executing vengeance on the unbelieving world.

§ 13. *There is no definite " end"*

That was not the kind of "coming" that this Gospel depicts or suggests. Doubtless, John regarded it as one

---

[1] See *Notes on N.T. Criticism* **2936** *a* on Westcott's suggestion of " some symbolic action," and on ἐπιστρέφω (R.V. " turn about ") :—

" If the narrative refers to a vision, to be taken separately from what precedes, then 'following' may denote literal symbolic 'following,' seen by Peter in that vision. After hearing and beginning to obey the call 'Follow me [to the cross]' Peter 'turns round,' in his vision, and sees the beloved disciple also 'following'—as indeed he did, according to tradition, to the very brink of death by martyrdom. Then he asks for a revelation of the future in store for his brother-apostle.

" Compare, however, Lk. xxii. 32. There, ἐπιστρέψας (preceding στήρισον τοὺς ἀδελφούς σου), applied to Peter, might indeed possibly be taken, as in Lk. i. 16, transitively ; but it is much more probably intransitive, 'having turned again,' and it suggests that there may have been various versions of an ambiguous tradition about Peter's 'turning again' after Christ's resurrection."

aspect of the truth. But he writes as if he believed that more than enough had been written about that aspect. He seems to be impatient of materialistic details—and especially of any that bordered on the theatrical—about the Lord's coming in a conquering, or royal, or imperial character, preferring to think of Him as entering into the heart of each believer, as into a friendly guest-chamber, so that the friend shall "sup" with Him and He with the friend[1].

Not even about the Ascension does John write in any definite way, or suggest a definite time when—much less a place where—it came to pass. "Touch me not," says the risen Saviour to Mary, "for I am not yet ascended to the Father." That is all, except a repetition implying that the Ascension is immediately impending: " Go unto my brethren and say to them I am [on the point of] ascending unto my Father and your Father." No subsequent mention of " ascending" is made in the rest of the Gospel. But some *data* appear, at first sight, given for inference. For whereas Jesus says here, " Touch me not, *for I am not yet* ascended," He says, eight days afterwards, to Thomas, " Put thy hand into my side." Is not the natural inference this, that since He could not be touched before by Mary because He had not ascended, but can be touched now by Thomas, therefore He is to be regarded as having ascended immediately after He spoke to Mary[2]?

---

[1] Comp. Rev. iii. 20.

[2] The earlier Christian Commentators explain that Mary was not worthy to "touch" Jesus because she did not " worship" Him as did the other women (Mt. xxviii. 9), who "took-hold-of (ἐκράτησαν) his feet." Westcott (on Jn xx. 17) says that " the exact form (μὴ ἅπτου) implies further that she was already clinging to Him when He spoke," and that it implies "the desire to retain." But does not Mt. xxviii. 9 "they took-hold-of his feet" imply "desire to retain"? Comp. Ignat. *Smyrn.* § 3 "Straightway they *grasped* (ἥψαντο) *Him* and believed."

It seems impossible to arrive at any safe conclusion about John's purpose except this, that he desires, without contradicting early and

But to say this, would have brought the Evangelist into direct contradiction of Luke, and perhaps of other traditions about the Ascension. Such a contradiction he avoids by not mentioning the subject again, and by bringing his Gospel to an end in such a way as to imply that there was no gulf of separation, scarcely even a line of demarcation, between the life of the risen Saviour with His disciples when He was on earth and when He was in heaven. Whether He is on earth or in heaven, He loves the disciples, and of His love there is no end.

This thought suggests a contrast between John and Matthew, whose last words do mention, if not an "end" exactly, at all events something like it, "I am with you alway, even unto *the accomplishment of the aeon*[1]." And this again suggests the question, "What has the Fourth Gospel to tell us elsewhere—since it tells us nothing here—about that *end of the world*, or *consummation of the aeon*, which Matthew speaks of, and which is alleged by some to have been a prominent subject of discourse with Jesus?" The answer may be given in two short statements about the verb, and the noun, "end." The verb is used twice, but only to denote what is "ended" on the Cross[2]. The noun is used only once—and that one instance how unsatisfactory to those who crave eschatological detail—"Having loved his own that were in the world, he loved them *unto the end*[3]."

This is the only "end" that John recognises, an end that is no end but rather a continuation of what always is and must be the same, the never-ending love of the Father. As

definite traditions concerning the time and place of Ascension, to leave room for a spiritual and indefinite belief in it.

[1] Mt. xxviii. 20 R.V. and A.V. "*the end of the world*." But R.V. marg. has "or, *the consummation of the age*."

[2] Jn xix. 28 "knowing that all things are now ended ($\tau\epsilon\tau\epsilon\lambda\epsilon\sigma\tau\alpha\iota$)," *ib.* 30 "it is ended ($\tau\epsilon\tau\epsilon\lambda\epsilon\sigma\tau\alpha\iota$)." Comp. Lk. xxii. 37 "that which [is] concerning me hath an end ($\tau\epsilon\lambda\sigma\varsigma$ $\epsilon\chi\epsilon\iota$)."

[3] Jn xiii. 1 R.V. marg. "or, *to the uttermost*."

for what seems to be the "end," the temporary departure of the Lord, it is only, John seems to say, "a little" difference —just as the Saviour Himself spoke of only "a little while" when He said, "A little while and ye behold me not, and again a little while and ye shall see me." Whether the Saviour is on earth or in heaven, He is henceforth in the heart of each beloved disciple, who can remember no more the sorrow "for the joy that a man is born into the world."

It is to "bear witness" to this "joy" and to this "birth," that the beloved disciple is called. Hence it is that he cannot be allowed to bear witness with his blood, like Peter—following the Lord gloriously and rapidly to heaven. Slow and less glorious (as some count glory) is to be his martyrdom, lingering on that he may bear witness, in the last of the Gospels, with what is called in the Johannine Epistles mere "ink and pen[1]."

And now that his work is finished, what is it after all? Nothing but a mere addition to the multitude of "books." Thus, in a deliberate bathos, "books," this Gospel terminates. It began in the infinite altitude of the Logos—the Word, through which the world was made. It has tried to describe that Word Incarnate, living, breathing, heard and handled by His disciples, the Lord in whose bosom the beloved disciple had once lain. It ends, as it were, in no end, letting the witnessing pen drop from the writer's hand as he finishes his book and reflects on its inadequacy. His friends come round him, encouraging him with an attestation of its truth. "We know that his witness is true." "Yes, true as far as it goes," he seems to reply, "but how far does it go? What avails a universe of 'books' in comparison with the Spirit

---

[1] It is interesting to note that the only books in the Bible that use the phrases "ink and pen" or "paper and ink" are Johannine Epistles (2 Jn 12, 3 Jn 13) and in both the thought is "I am unwilling to use these things unless I am obliged. How much better is it to speak 'face to face'!"

of the Word? If all the true things about the Word could be written down in 'books,' book after book, they would go on being written till 'the world itself would not hold them.'"

But whom do we mean by "the writer" from whose hands we speak of the "pen" as "dropping"? If he is not the aged Apostle, but only the Apostle's representative or interpreter, is not this expression quite out of place?

Not quite, if we may suppose some special circumstances, which appear to accord with the special character of the text. It would be natural and necessary that, during the last years of the preaching of the Johannine gospel by the Johannine interpreter, there would be rarer and rarer interchanges of vigorous and continuous thought between the old man and his disciple. Among such interchanges, a saying like the one we are considering—reiterated perhaps even to monotony toward the conclusion of the Apostle's life—might naturally be treasured up by his interpreter and appended, after his death, to the work published in his name. For indeed the words sound like a reflection that might be repeated over and over again by a very old man—at the close of a life crowded with experiences of strange unutterable things, visible and invisible, things of this world, and things of the world to come—comparing his mingled recollections of the whole with present inadequate attempts to describe this or that particular part or particular aspect, and harping on their inadequacy.

Jerome tells us that when John had scarcely strength enough to be carried into the church at Ephesus and say a few words, he repeated "Little children, love one another" so often that "the disciples and brethren" were "a little tired of it (taedio affecti)[1]." Somewhat similarly we may suppose that when the aged Apostle had passed even beyond that stage of weakness, and when the gospel, long preached in his name, and now at last committed to writing, was brought to him on

---

[1] Jerome (on Gal. vi. 10).

his deathbed to receive his blessing, he once more repeated his disparaging criticism of books. Most appropriately would it be set down here by the Apostle's disciple and representative, the actual author of the Gospel—after his Master's death, or during the last days of his extreme and decrepit old age—as expressing both what John himself was in the habit of saying about books in general, and what John's disciple now felt about his own book in particular (though he had done his utmost to make it spiritually faithful) when sending it forth to the world as the Gospel of the Disciple whom Jesus loved[1].

---

[1] For a somewhat similar saying of Papias, mentioning "books," but using "voice" where the Johannine writer would probably use "word," see Euseb. iii. 39. 4 οὐ γὰρ τὰ ἐκ τῶν βιβλίων τοσοῦτόν με ὠφελεῖν ὑπελάμβανον ὅσον τὰ παρὰ ζώσης φωνῆς καὶ μενούσης. Also Irenaeus (iii. 2. 1) quotes a saying of heretics about "scriptures," that the truth cannot be extracted from them by those who are ignorant of tradition, "non enim per literas traditam illam sed per *vivam vocem*."